Helping Your Teenager Succeed in School

Dorothy and Lyle Williams

Family Tree™ Group®

Loveland, Colorado

Helping Your Teenager Succeed In School

Copyright © 1989 by Search Institute

First Printing

Credits
Edited by Eugene C. Roehlkepartain
Illustrated by Steve Elde
Designed by Judy Atwood

Excerpts from *The Quicksilver Years: The Hopes and Fears of Early Adolescence* by Peter Benson, Dorothy Williams and Arthur Johnson. Copyright © 1987 by Search Institute, Inc. Reprinted with permission of Harper & Row, Publishers, Inc.

Scripture quotations are from the Holy Bible, New International Version. Copyright © 1973, 1978, 1984 International Bible Society. Used by permission of Zondervan Bible Publishers.

ISBN 0-931529-63-8
Printed in the United States of America

For Beth, Roger and Holly
because of
all we have learned
through them.

ACKNOWLEDGMENTS

A great many people have helped in this book's formation—some intentionally, and others entirely unwittingly. Lee Sparks at Group Books first asked whether we had a book in mind, and Cindy Hansen helped shape the initial outline. The staff at Search Institute—principally its president, Peter Benson—put up with some shortened work hours on Dorothy's part and gave us the run of the library and word-processing equipment.

Gene Roehlkepartain's editorial insights and his gift for coherence and organization—combined with a gracious willingness to hear and allow for occasional divergent viewpoints—have been invaluable in shaping the book in its final form.

And thousands of students and parents have, over the years, opened to us their anxieties, failures, successes and dreams—whether in the classroom, in the counselor's office, in evening classes, at church or over the back fence. Their stories and insights have broadened and deepened our current understanding of the real meaning of success.

CONTENTS

 CHAPTER 1

Can You Really Make a Difference?

Every parent knows the moment. The outside door opens and closes. The footsteps cross the floor toward you, and your teenager holds out a scrap of paper. The report card. Seeing it, you're full of interest. But, at the same instant, you feel a moment of dread. You draw breath and hesitate. Then you look.

There on the card you find, in a familiar code, a cryptic judgment on many hours of your teenager's life—hours of concentrated effort; hours, sometimes, of real struggle. And, in some indefinable way, the grades seem like a judgment on you, as well.

Whether you realize it or not, "report card day" tells a great deal about how you and your teenager handle the stresses on each of you. The report card and your reactions to it symbolize how well you cope with the demanding business of being a teenager's parent and how successfully the teenager copes with the conflicting pressures he or she faces. Every time your teenager's report card arrives, important—though unspoken—questions underlie the event:

● Is your teenager showing signs of success in moving toward the maturity and responsibility that adulthood will demand?

● Can you give your teenager the freedom both to succeed and to fail—and thus learn?

● Does either of you know how deeply you are involved in fulfilling each other's dreams?

🍎 The Challenge of School

For both teenagers and parents, many of the satisfactions and disappointments of the teenage years revolve around the teenager's school experience. Concern about school performance topped a list of 20 worries ranked by young adolescents in a Search Institute study.[1] Parents share the concern. An informal survey of parents of teenagers found that their overwhelming concerns about their teenagers were peer pressure and grades.[2]

The teenage years produce the most troubling changes in children as well as the most severe challenges to the parent-child relationship. One of parents' greatest needs is to know how to deal compassionately and successfully with their changing teenager. The changes bring lots of questions about education:

● "My daughter is pulling away from me, yet I know she still needs help in school. How much should I push?"

● "Our eldest son loves school. But our youngest son is fighting it every step of the way. What should I do about his foot-dragging?"

● "What grades can I expect from my child?"

● "How involved should I be in my teenager's learning?"

● "What will happen when my daughter is exposed to ideas and lifestyles that conflict with ours?"

To answer these specific questions about education, we have to begin by answering some of the perennial and basic questions of being a teenager's parent: Is what I'm experiencing as a parent normal? Do I still have any influence on my teenager? Is it too late for me to do anything that matters?

Parents Do Make a Difference

While teenagers are certainly searching for their own identity during adolescence, they still need their parents. And parents continue to influence their child's choices, behaviors and attitudes toward school and life. Education experts repeatedly declare that parents are absolutely central to their child's education. Consider the following quotes:

● "Parents are their children's first and most influential teachers," a U.S. Department of Education report declares. "What parents do to help their children learn is more important to academic success than how well-off the family is."[3]

● Psychologist Bruno Bettelheim adds, "The essential ingredient in most children's success in school is a positive relation to his parents and to their involvement in intellectual matters."[4]

● And in the U.S. Department of Education report, *A Nation at Risk*, the committee members admonished parents: "As surely as you are your child's first and most influential teacher, your child's ideas about education and its significance begin with you . . . Above all, exhibit a commitment to continued learning in your own life."[5]

As these quotations indicate, educators and psychologists alike believe parents are pivotal influences in their teenagers' education. As you read this book and seek to help your teenager, keep this perspective firmly in mind. Just because your teenager now refuses to acknowledge your influence doesn't mean you don't have any. Teenagers don't control most forces that work toward their education. They control only their cooperation and the enthusiasm with which they receive that education. The rest comes as a gift, evidence of the grace of God—though only the wisest among them realize it at the time.

Parents are involved in their teenagers' education much more deeply than most of them recognize. Involvement during the elementary years is practically universal, of course. It's a rare parent who hasn't flipped flashcards, read spelling words or checked arithmetic for an elementary child. But by the time that child becomes a teenager, most parents believe that they no longer have any influence on their child's education and that other than helping to finance however many years of education are still ahead, they're out of their child's educational picture.

Nothing could be further from the truth. Teenagers continue to need their parents' interest, involvement and support. They won't usually ask for it, but they need it. Your opinion matters a great deal to your teenager.

So does your simply being there. Too many parents are convinced that their teenagers have turned entirely against them. But children from good, supportive homes usually haven't turned against their parents at all. A child who has always been happy and secure at home is nurtured by the secret knowledge that home is still there as a support base or safety net ready to provide a soft landing in case of disaster.

A Search Institute study asked 8,000 fifth- through ninth-graders about the importance of 24 different life goals. The top life goal for these young people turned out to be "to have a happy family life." And the fifth-ranked goal (a respectable ranking—far above "looking good to other kids," "being popular" or "having lots of money") was "to make my parents proud of me."[6]

Make no mistake. Your teenagers need you as they learn and grow. To be sure, they're passing through a developmental stage in which the major task is to find their own identity, so they have to create distance between themselves and you. But they haven't stopped caring that you're there. What feels to you like rejection is probably nothing more than your teenager's need for a little distance to gain perspective.

You play an important role in your teenager's life, and your opinions are crucial. Remember, high—very high—on young people's priority list is "to make my parents proud of me." Unfortunately, while teenagers indicate this priority on surveys, sometimes they don't show it at home.

🍎 Humility: The Lesson of Parenthood

Parenthood is a continuing education in humility. True, it's also one of life's greatest adventures—filled with love, learning and lots of laughter. But it *is* an education in humility. Of course, since humility is a major Christian virtue (1 Peter 5:5-6), such an education might reasonably be considered a blessing. But it never feels like one.

C.S. Lewis says that if we met a truly humble person, we'd probably notice only that the person seemed cheerful, intelligent and reasonably interested in what we had to say. And, further, "If you do dislike him it will be because you feel a little envious of anyone who seems to enjoy life so easily. He will not be thinking about humility: he will not be thinking about himself at all."[7]

Humility is self-forgetfulness. It's at the opposite extreme of the maturity scale from self-consciousness. It's so interested in other people's welfare that it sometimes forgets whether its hair is combed or whether it has taken time for lunch. Those who demonstrate it are the "poor in spirit" to whom Jesus said the kingdom of heaven belongs (Matthew 5:3).

Parenthood repeatedly reminds us how little we know even of our own children and how much mystery there is in life. When our daughter's health is threatened or her friendships go wrong, we discover again how helpless we are to protect her from life's inevitable ills and hurts. As she grows older, we learn the further humbling lesson that we must gradually loosen our ties to this person in whom we've invested so much time and love, and let her go.

A parent's lessons in humility begin at birth and continue, in various forms, throughout life. The lesson proceeds with each tiny step children take as they grow. When your baby boy learns to hold a spoon to feed himself, he doesn't need you to feed him anymore. When he learns to talk, he no longer needs you to guess what he needs; he can tell you. When your daughter runs to greet her favorite babysitter with a delighted squeal, you know her world has grown beyond the point where you have her exclusive affection. In small, everyday steps such as these, parents learn that they're less powerful and more dispensable than they once thought. These are the lessons of humility.

Parents generally respond to these lessons of humility in one of three ways. Some bow to the lessons, overlearning them. Others resist the lessons, refusing to accept evidence of their own limited power.

But other parents embrace humility's lesson—the lesson of ownership. They truly believe that their child is a gift from God (Psalm 127:3). And they allow this belief to deepen their understanding of God's grace. As a result, they live in a charming and joyful state of humility—continually poor in spirit, continually blessed.

These parents understand that the child is not, finally, theirs. It doesn't even occur to them to take credit for their child's nature or accomplishments. Their son or daughter is someone they know extremely well and love beyond all reason. But, in talking to these parents, you get the impression that they have little awareness of having had a part in what their child has grown up to be. They appear honestly to believe that the child has been, from birth onward, a gift from God.

Identity: The Challenge of Adolescence

Looking back, teenagers sometimes feel nostalgic about the simplicity of the elementary school years. By the age of 11 or 12, most children convey an air of calm and self-confidence. They seem comfortable with their identity and at home in the world. When they run into trouble, they usually turn to their parents for suggestions, and soon life flows smoothly again.

But then things change. Life gets much more complicated. The physical developments of puberty begin, along with the first awareness of sexual attraction. At about the same time, many school systems require a change to a junior high school. Young teenagers find themselves thrust into a place where the day's structure is different, the routines and rules more complicated and the subjects harder. Everyone seems to expect a lot more of them.

Now they face all kinds of new problems and puzzles. The old comfort with their personal identity is gone; the old at-home-in-the-world air is less visible; and a new search for identity begins. For some teenagers, these new pressures and attractions seriously interfere with education.

Watching some teenagers during these changes, you'd think their chief aim in life is to teach their parents humility . . . for the wrong reasons, of course. Their intended message comes close to the 4-year-old's taunt: "You're not the boss of me!" They're struggling to prove their capacity to be in charge of their own lives, make their own decisions, act independently, run the show by themselves.

In their search for their own identity, in their over-eagerness to gain some self-convincing distance from their parents, teenagers sometimes do things that hurt.

Most parents find comfort in knowing that the sudden appearance in their teenager of a steely self-will and an insistence on privacy aren't signs of problems but are normal elements of the adolescent search for identity and independence. It's comforting to know that their teenager's changes are essentially like those in other teenagers, and that much of what goes on in their family is going on in other families too.

🍎 *Parents Who Perceive Problems*

You may be reading this book feeling a sense of urgency. You know that something between you and your teenager has changed, and you feel stress and anxiety about your teenager's attitudes and school performance. But you aren't sure exactly what's wrong. And you don't know whether there's anything you can do to improve things.

In these cases, you need to begin by asking yourself

some of these questions that may already be on your mind:

- How does my concern now compare to my concern during my child's elementary school experience? Is it more? less? about the same? If there's a difference, what does it tell me?

- How do my teenager's grades compare with my grades at that age? Do I think they should be comparable? What does the comparison tell me about my own expectations?

- Is my teenager's concern about grades more, less or about the same as mine? How can I interpret the similarity or difference?

- Am I looking for a way to get my teenager to buckle down in school? If so, what's my motivation?

- How much responsibility do I think my teenager's teachers ought to bear for my teenager's learning? How much do I think belongs to me?

- How much of my own reputation is wrapped up in my teenager's grades? Can I acknowledge that to myself or to anyone else?

Parents Who Seek Insights

You may be reading this book more to discover whether there's a way to improve how you deal with your teenager's education. In this case, you may not have felt much stress as your child has entered the teenage years. Changes have occurred, but you have no strong, anxiety-producing sense that your basic relationship with your child is in trouble. Yet you've heard enough from people with older children to wonder whether there may be trouble down the road. It would be a good idea, you think, to be prepared. You may want to examine these kinds of questions:

- Should (or did) my role in my child's school life radically change when he or she enters (or entered) secondary school?

- Am I cheating my teenager by not stressing grades

enough? Do a few well-placed incentives really help teenagers achieve?

● How can I step back and "let go," while, at the same time, let my teenager know I care about school life?

● Should I initiate contact with the school? Or should I wait until someone comes to me?

● What goals do I have in mind for my teenager during high school? And afterward? What do these expectations say about me?

● How much voice should I have in my teenager's academic choices?

In successive chapters of this book, we'll suggest some answers to both sets of questions. To do this, we must examine new territory as well as some that will seem familiar. We'll suggest concrete things you can do to help your teenager study more effectively, organize school responsibilities more usefully and deal with anxiety about tests. We'll also offer some new ways of thinking about your child's schooling.

Like the teenagers Search Institute surveyed, we think a happy family life is extremely important. And we long for parents and teenagers to find and hold onto the kind of relationship that makes their life together not only productive but full of joy.

 CHAPTER 2

What's So Important About Grades?

What are grades good for?

The question may come as a surprise. Why even bother to ask it? For so long grades have been a fixed part of education that you might as well ask what the pyramids or Labor Day or Gibraltar are good for. They're simply there.

However, the question is important. For, in exploring some answers, we also uncover some things grades are *not* good for. In the process, we gain a more realistic perspective on grades.

Pervasive though they are throughout all of education, it's hard to find anyone who really likes grades. Nearly everyone agrees that grades are an inadequate vehicle for a complicated and significant message. And yet grades persist. We can't be entirely comfortable with them, but we apparently can't do without them, either.

Learning is what's really important about education. Grades are, at best, symbols, issued from time to time to represent the learning that has been taking place. Grades can't *do* anything for you—any more than a gas gauge can make the car move. It's what's in the tank that makes the car move; the gauge only provides a pointer to what is available for use.

Teachers are interested, first and foremost, in helping young people develop their minds and learning skills. They want to help students feel competent and worthwhile, and they seek to foster in learners attributes of maturity that will help them throughout life. However, such long-term goals are usually approached through the mundane process of assigning reading, requiring homework, asking questions, conducting discussions, giving tests and, yes, assigning grades.

Just as most students don't like grades, most teachers would prefer not to give grades. They prefer teaching to grading, and they'd rather spend their energy developing new, more effective ways to help students learn. But they assign grades because no one has discovered a better indicator of progress.

Teachers don't like giving grades for several reasons:

● They know a single grade doesn't say enough. Teachers would much rather sit down with a student and parent to talk about their observations of the student's progress in learning.

● They fear inaccuracy. Some teachers dread assigning grades because some judgment error on a borderline situation could inflict hurt or cause anxiety that's out of proportion to the grade's importance.

● They aren't absolutely certain that every grade they give is fair. Most high school teachers work with 150 or more students every day, and, try as they do to know each one, it's hard to know exactly how each student is progressing.

● Knowing what they do about the learning process, teachers aren't always sure their measurement techniques are adequate. It's simply impossible to measure adequately the complex learning process with a few brief paper-and-pencil tests.

How Teachers Assign Grades

Whatever our judgments about their fairness or usefulness, it makes sense to know how teachers assign grades. Grading systems vary—even within a given school.

Although some schools have specific grading guidelines, most principals allow teachers to work out their own grading systems.

It's perfectly reasonable to ask any of your teenager's teachers what system they use. When you do, you're most likely to hear one of two responses: (1) The teacher has developed some preset standards for grades that often remain the same from year to year; or (2) the teacher issues grades on some modification of the normal curve. Let's look at these systems:

Preset standard. "Mastery learning," a concept that gained prominence during the 1980s, is one of the most popular grading methods using preset standards. The system is based on the belief that all students should know, for example, how to add, subtract, multiply and divide whole numbers by the time they reach a certain grade in school. Students are tested for this particular mastery. Most will "pass" the preset standard, and those who don't pass will receive remedial instruction to help them master those skills.

Some educational computer programs use principles similar to mastery learning. They are programmed so that, for example, a student can't go on to subtraction until the preceding steps of addition are fully mastered.

It might seem, at first, that requiring students to meet a preset standard is fair. Why not require a certain percentage of answers correct for an A, a lesser percentage for a B, and so on?

However, such a system is seldom satisfactory, for it doesn't take into account several important factors: the difficulty of the material being tested, the effectiveness of the teaching and surrounding circumstances that affect learning.

● Sometimes students know exactly what will be on a test before it's given—as in the case of a spelling test or a quiz on the capitals of the 50 states. For tests such as these, giving a passing grade for answering correctly only 75 percent of the questions is probably too lenient. By contrast, the 75 percent passing requirement may be too stiff for a three-week social studies unit test that covers two lengthy and fact-filled chapters in the textbook.

● Whenever an entire class does more poorly than usual, the first question the teacher must ask is whether the material was adequately presented. Students shouldn't be penalized because the teacher failed to communicate material adequately.

● Numerous other factors can also interfere with the business of learning, accounting for variations in test scores. These factors could include absence of an unusually large number of students at crucial points, presence of a substitute teacher on a given day, the weather, or the anticipation of an important athletic or dramatic event. Though teachers may wish education could continue regardless of surrounding circumstances, in reality it doesn't.

Modified curve. Because of the limitations of preset grading scales, many teachers prefer to assign grades using some modification of the normal curve. The term "modification" is important. Strictly speaking, the normal curve would provide for as many F's as A's, a somewhat larger but equal number of B's and D's, and C's for more than a third of the class. However, almost nobody grades that way. Instead, teachers make judgments—which is generally a good thing.

Most teachers resort to some modification of the strict curve. Typically, the teachers will put test points or cumulative points from a term on a distribution from highest to lowest. Then they will assign grades according to the form of the distribution. Natural breaks often occur that help define the cutoff points for particular grades. The distribution of scores on a 50-point test might look like Diagram 1 for a class of 30 students.

Some teachers prefer not to assign letter grades for individual assignments and tests. Instead, they accumulate points throughout the term and place the overall total on a final distribution. Based on this distribution, they assign letter grades only once for the entire term.

In general, students see this method as particularly fair.

Diagram 1
Modified Curve

Score	Number of Students	Grade
50		
49		A
48	2	
47	1	
46		
45	1	B
44	4	
43	3	
42	5	
41	5	C
40	3	
39	2	
38		
37	1	D
36	2	
35		
34		
33		
32		
31	1	F

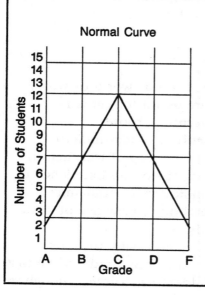

Normal Curve

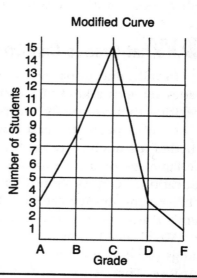

Modified Curve

It eliminates the agony of "just missing a B on the last three tests." Students know that the final grade will be figured on their total points earned during the term. Even the student who just missed a B on three tests may still, on the cumulative point distribution, qualify for the desired B.

Every grading method has philosophical problems. For example, is a student who gets an F for answering only 31 of 50 questions correctly a "failure" in the teacher's eyes? the parent's? God's? After all, the student did learn and retain 31 facts or concepts worth testing. And yet, it's reasonable to ask if a student whose score is significantly below all others *should* pass.

The opposite question arises when assigning grades to an enriched or accelerated class. To qualify for these classes at all, students have already proved unusual ability. How shall grades be assigned to them? For example, the curve is the wrong instrument when the requirement for getting into Art III is to complete Art I and II with A grades. For that advanced class, issuing A's to everyone is probably fair.

The matter of assigning grades is complicated. Yet despite their limitations, grades do have their uses. There are also some highly important things they're not good for. Let's look at what grades do and don't do.

What Grades Can Do

In our educational world and in our world of work, grades serve as a kind of measure useful for certain specific—though usually short-term—purposes.

Grades point toward learning. Grades indicate whether a student is ready for a next step of learning. In the language of the National Commission on Excellence in Education, "Grades should be indicators of academic achievement so they can be relied on as evidence of a student's readiness for further study."[1]

We all need measuring sticks—especially for those things (such as learning) that are invisible. Grades serve that purpose. They tell whether a student has learned enough in

French I to be ready to move on to French II. They are your protection, as a parent, from seeing your child placed in a class where struggle and failure are inevitable. They provide one criterion for placing students in accelerated courses or allowing advanced placement in college. And they help determine which students need special tutoring in certain subjects.

Grades motivate students. We've all heard the reluctant learner's lament: "I gotta study. I've got a test tomorrow, and I haven't read this stuff." A lot of people are convinced that most kids would never crack a book nor attend a lecture if they didn't have to earn a decent grade. Grades represent both the carrot and the stick, the prize and the prod.

Goaded to action by the pursuit of a particular grade, a student sometimes discovers interesting nuggets that eventually draw him or her into hard work. Then the work is done no longer for the grade but for the joy of learning.

At the same time, the relationship of motivation, grades and achievement is complex. Nobody has thus far been able to figure out exactly what it is.[2] It's easy to believe that grades motivate young people who get A's and B's. But they seem to have little motivating effect on teenagers who have become accustomed to seeing D's and F's.

Grades help students get into college. The education community has chosen to use the symbolic power of grades as an entry fee. Most colleges consider the high school grade point average as the major factor for admission—although they all emphasize that they look at a number of other factors as well. Thus grades can make a major difference in your teenager's future.

Grades help with financial assistance. Parents who urge their children toward higher grades because of particular benefits correctly estimate the value of grades for scholarships. The father who cautions his son, "You've got to get those grades up or you're not going to be eligible for a football scholarship," is at least partially right.

Grades provide a measuring stick for granting both

athletic and non-athletic scholarships. Just ask Erin's parents. Erin wants to go to one of her denomination's colleges. She has been accepted to her chosen college, but the sum total of her high school grades leaves her three percentage points below the college's scholarship cutoff. The substance of education (as distinguished from the grade symbol) is important to Erin's parents. But they're discovering—at a cost of several thousand dollars—that good grades can "pay" at college entrance time.

Another financial benefit of grades is the practice of some car insurance companies that lower their premiums for teenage drivers with high grades.

Grades help with job-hunting. Grades are often important when you're job-hunting. In deciding whether to hire a person, some employers examine school records, taking into account the record of attendance, record of tardiness and the grade point average.

Grades help prepare for adult life. School is the teenager's main work, and most parents believe that school success is a prelude to success in life. Whatever your definition of success, this perspective makes school and grades serious business.

Proponents of grading point out that we live in a competitive world. We're classified by a job title, that, in turn, determines our position in the salary scale. Just as grades aren't always fair or just, neither are salaries or promotions. But hierarchies of compensation, winning and losing, A's and F's, are part of the real world. So young people might as well learn how to deal with competition.

Grades affirm some young people. For some teenagers, grades can fulfill a less quantifiable but useful purpose in affirming teenagers' sense of significance and competence.

One of the major questions teenagers try to settle as they mature is "How much do I matter?" Few teenagers are confident that they're really important to anyone, and in competition they can test their significance. The school experience offers a great many opportunities for finding a

WHAT'S SO IMPORTANT ABOUT GRADES? **27**

place in the hierarchy.

Because of the way they're assigned, grades can provide at least temporary status—an indication of the student's location on the achievement ladder. Test by test, term by term, students see themselves ranked against one another.

Of course, other areas of teenagers' lives also yield winners and losers. Your teenager is chosen for the lead in the school musical, or he or she is not. The chosen one is a winner, and all others—some of them desperately eager for the part—are losers. In athletic competition, some teenagers are chosen for the first team. The rest are relegated to the second-best team, whatever its name, or they warm the bench. Some teenagers hit home runs. Others strike out.

For teenagers who win, such competitive activities are highly affirming. Many quiet, studious young people who lack the charisma and social skills that most teenagers prize have had their sense of personal significance abundantly bolstered by discovering and exercising the academic, artistic or athletic skill with which they're blessed.

🍎 What Grades Don't Do

While grades certainly have important functions in our educational system, they don't do everything we sometimes ascribe to them. Here are some examples:

Grades don't guarantee success. Despite their importance in some areas of life, good grades don't guarantee success as an adult. What was your pastor's high school grade point average? What kind of college grades did your doctor get? your barber? Have you ever asked about a political candidate's grades—no matter how humble the position at stake? Do they really matter anymore?

A mature adult's worth shows in such qualities as perception, professional competence, personal warmth, honesty, integrity and commitment to the welfare of others. With the possible exception of professional competence,

"But Mom, Albert Einstein didn't do well in school either."

academic brilliance doesn't predict any of these qualities. Ten years out of school, grades are more of a curiosity than a measuring stick. Like the dried, faded prom corsage, they no longer carry the significance they did when fresh—nor the power to impress.

A string of straight A's throughout high school or a 4.0 record in college never performed life-sustaining surgery nor taught a child to read nor patiently helped a grieving family back to health and faith. Good grades never wrote a play nor threw a touchdown pass nor offered an intercessory prayer.

People do these things. People, with all their diverse talents, deficiencies, interests, wants, needs, quirks and vulnerabilities. People, who train, educate and nurture their God-given gifts for such works and wonders. You can probably think of several marvelous human beings you know who never in their lives earned an A in any school subject.

On the other hand, you probably also knew academically brilliant people who garnered fistfuls of A's with apparent ease. But when you encountered some of these people years later at a class reunion or in an airport somewhere, they turned out to be disappointments—brazen egotists or self-absorbed and garrulous, or all squashy-plump and complacent.

One reason grades are important is that they give some indication of the likelihood of success in later life. But they aren't guarantees.

Grades don't help everyone. Like every hierarchy, grading scales have a bottom as well as a top. The people who wind up time after time at the bottom are just as vulnerable, just as eager to succeed, just as easily discouraged as the people at the top. As a result, some develop protective shells so they can pretend that D's and F's don't hurt. But they do.

Some people aren't born with the skills and aptitudes that suit them well for academic learning. One of the things grades emphatically do *not* do is measure a person's worth. However, when grades are assigned during our culture's long educational apprenticeship, some infinitely valuable young people will constantly receive the message that they're less able than others, less apt, less competent, of less worth.

Teenagers are just beginning to search out their identity and worth. They need some of the symbols of success to gauge their value. But many of them learn, early on, that they'd better not look for those gauges in school; it simply isn't their game. And since school takes so much of every teenager's time and attention, the grading hierarchies work against helping these teenagers develop a conviction of their worth.

Someone else must see those teenagers' worth, and then help them see it themselves. George Olsen, a master teacher widely regarded as the patron saint of our local high school, teaches 50 students who have been defined as on the verge of dropping out. He agonizes over what the "failure" label does to his students. "I hate giving grades," he says. "We work so hard, day after day, to help open up a little bit of light for these kids, to help them feel good about themselves, but the system demands that we give grades and pound their fragile egos into the ground again."

Our friend Ron teaches auto mechanics at a vocational school. He says that many of his students enter the program primed for failure. Over the years they've learned to expect being classified with the "no-brain crowd," and they demonstrate in their hostile, sullen or macho behaviors that they expect to be classified as failures in his classes too.

Yet most of these young people are neither stupid nor incompetent. Ron tells us that, almost overnight, some of these convinced failures become motivated, enthusiastic learners. What changes? They're introduced to hands-on skills they understand and care about, and they have a teacher who cares about them, knows how to teach and respects their right to succeed.

There are those for whom grades will always symbolize being a loser. If your teenager isn't cut out to be a scholar, one of the best things you can do is to search for the places where he or she can succeed. And pray that sometime during your teenager's schooling someone like Ron or George will be there to help.

Grades shouldn't be tools to bolster parents.
Sometimes parents use their teenager's grades to validate their own role as parents. Teenagers who bring home good grades bear witness that their parents have done something right, and that's highly important to some parents. Their children's grades serve some families as a way of keeping up with the Joneses. They carefully clip published honor roll lists, post them in a prominent place and preserve them along with other cherished family mementos.

Parents should guard against allowing their loving, appreciative response to a child's success to turn into a prop for their own egos. If they carry their celebration of their child's achievements too far, they risk unintentionally amusing their friends. They also run the risk of taking psychological ownership of their teenager's school performance—with all of the potential problems that taking ownership can bring.

Grades can be misused as keys to belonging.
Sometimes people misuse good grades as a condition of psychological membership. Jody's family is this way. Unless Jody gets an A, it's not good enough. Jody's family is used to coming in first, being at the top of the heap, carrying off the honors. Dad is chief of staff at a hospital. Mom has been top real estate seller two years in a row. Jody is not naturally a quick learner, but she is resigned to spending long, hard hours studying so she can keep her grades up. Asked about it, she shrugs resignedly and says: "I've got to. They expect it."

 The he Greatest Danger

We live in a world in which competition seems inevitable. It's the students with straight-A transcripts whose applications for admission are welcomed at the more prestigious colleges. It's the all-state athletes in major competitive sports who are courted by major universities—and whose financial worries seem magically to disappear after they choose a school.

It's the students who earn 3.9 and 4.0 g.p.a.s in college who have their pick of high-paying, prestigious jobs—if, that is, they decide to turn down the variety of graduate school scholarships, assistantships or other inducements to continue their competitive efforts in academia.

In short, to them who hath shall be given—or so it seems.

So who are we to question your desire to see that your teenager earns membership among them who hath?

Keep in mind, we're not against high grades. We cheered enthusiastically when our children brought them home. But we didn't *demand* them. We did expect effort that wisely used their own talents and the learning opportunities they were offered.

The problem with grades begins when parents, in their insistence on performance, make top grades the priority of growing up. They make the mistake of elevating symbols (grades) on high as objects of worship. Grades become idols on which we focus our attention, energy and dreams. Of course we want good things for ourselves and our children; we believe God does too. But we slip into idolatry when our desire for the good thing (high grades) becomes the fuel that drives everything else.

We all know what idolatry is, of course:

● It's the subject of the First Commandment: "You shall have no other gods before me" (Exodus 20:3).

● It's given very unsympathetic mention by both major and minor prophets, who tended to attach words like "woe" and "destruction" and "pollution" to it.

● It's defined in Paul's letter to the Colossians either as greed or covetousness, depending on the translation (Colossians 3:5).

A modern theologian defines idolatry as "giving uncritical allegiance to human constructs that can never be worthy of uncritical allegiance."[3] If ever there were a human construct, it's high grades. Very human. They're assigned to human teenagers by human adults on evaluation of a given body of human work.

The question is: Have grades become an idol to you? How much is it costing you to see that your teenager gets the grades you think he or she ought to have? If it's not costing in literal dollars and cents, then is it expensive in personal anxiety, in strain on your relationship with your teenager, and in peace and quiet around the house?

In order to evaluate your involvement in your teenager's education, you need to search deeper. What are your goals for your teenager? What worries drive you? And what value do you place on academic and economic success as opposed to giving back to God the best you can foster in your child?

Difficult questions. But idolatry has such cleverly seductive ways of insinuating itself into our conversations, assumptions, hopes and values that we may be able to see it only when we answer difficult questions. The prevailing culture surrounds us so constantly that it's almost a full-time job to keep track of the ways we inadvertently accept society's point of view as our own. When we recognize that acceptance, we know we're off course.

The Source of Real Significance

Grades are useful symbols for some areas of life. But they are inadequate measures of our significance and our sense of self. Grades become most dangerous when people wrap up their identity (or their child's identity) in the letters on a report card.

When you and your teenager are deeply convinced that you are part of God's family, then the symbols of day-to-day victory over others have less significance. Your ultimate identity is securely fixed. But not many teenagers have that conviction. Eric Hoffer, in *The Ordeal of Change*, suggests that we need things that bolster our pride when we do not have the assurances within us that we are somebody. And, he says, "If we cannot have the originals, we can never have enough of the substitutes."[4]

Because the scramble for signs of significance is all around us, it's hard to keep our true identity in mind. But in the Christian family, we need to remind each other of our lasting identity and significance. When the pressure to excel against difficult odds makes us anxious, we need to help each other remember who, finally, we are and to whom we ultimately belong.

Like the rest of us, teenagers need to hear that reminder often. Unlike grades that inadequately measure short-term, limited progress, our true identity and significance have a transcendent, eternal importance.

 CHAPTER 3

What Motivates Your Teenager?

Gina cares a lot about her school performance. Just ask her. "She's always *talking* about what she has to do for school," a friend explains. "It's just that she never seems to get to *doing* any of it."

What Gina does do is look in mirrors. If no mirror is handy, she constantly checks her reflection in windows or in the glass in picture frames. Sure, she worries about school. But two other things concern her much more—how she looks and how well others like her. These concerns are so intense for Gina that her schoolwork occupies only the outermost fringes of her consciousness.

If a teacher stops Gina in the hall to talk, her eyes never meet the adult's eyes. It's not that she's too shy to make eye contact; she's just preoccupied with watching her classmates pass, anxious to see whether they notice her, wondering if they conclude that she's in trouble since she's talking to a teacher.

In fact, she often *is* in trouble. She's always late for classes. If the tardy bell rings when she's in the bathroom arranging her hair (a regular between-class ritual), she sacrifices the classroom time without a flutter of distress. She's also exhaustively creative in inventing excuses to avoid submitting her hair to the ruinous experience of immersion in the swimming pool during physical education.

Not even rock-bottom grades in gym will induce her to sur-
render protective custody of her appearance. If she can't
get her mother to write a note certifying she has a sore
throat, she visits the school nurse, claiming various vague
and complicated symptoms. Sometimes she simply spends
the hour doing advanced hair-arranging in the bathroom.

At home Gina spends hours on the phone checking her
friends' perceptions of what happened that day, so she
rarely has time for homework. Although she regularly
writes several-pages-long notes to her friends, she rarely
manages to complete written assignments for English.

After a week at school, Gina devotes her weekends to
cruising the shopping mall, meeting this friend or that,
checking out the fashion shops, seeing and being seen. It's
a demanding regimen, but she sticks faithfully to it—
despite considerable pressure from adults (and even some
friends) to change.

Her parents say they've tried everything to get their
daughter to improve her schoolwork. Her mother has
threatened to reduce Gina's allowance if she doesn't study
more. And the last time report cards came out, her father
sat Gina down for a good talking-to. "Gina, these are a
disgrace," he said, tossing the report card into her lap dis-
dainfully. "I want you to cut out so much fooling around
with those friends of yours. Your mother and I want to see
some better grades next term. If you don't get down to
some serious homework, there's going to be real trouble
around here."

Gina looked penitent. She'd try, she said. And for about
a week she did carry books home, and she did study a
little. But then the phone would ring, the conversations
would go on and on, and hope for real improvement in
Gina's next grades began to fade.

It may help us understand what's going on with Gina
and her parents—and in our relations with our own
teenagers—if we understand a little more of what lies
beneath the surface of our daily doings and observations.

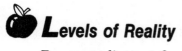 # Levels of Reality

Everyone lives at four levels of reality. Though we're usually conscious of only one level, all four shape who we are and what we do. At the uppermost level and claiming most of our conscious attention is behavior. At succeeding deeper levels are our motivations, values and spiritual identity (Diagram 2, "Levels of Reality").

When we move deeper through the levels and come to understand them, we find that each level profoundly influences all the levels above it. By examining all four levels and becoming conscious of them, we can develop a better understanding of our teenagers—and perhaps ourselves.

Diagram 2
Levels of Reality

Behavior
Motivations
Values
Spiritual Identity

Behavior—What We Do and Say

The behavior level is the one most immediately acces-
sible to us. It claims our attention most of the time because
it's the level where we most easily and naturally observe
others. For example, we hear our teenagers talking to
friends on the telephone:

● Defiantly: "I don't *care* what old Simpson said. I'm
not going to do a stupid outline of that whole chapter. I
already know what's in there."

● Pleadingly: "Isn't 7:30 too early to get up on a
Saturday? It's the only sleep-in morning I have."

We also hear our teenagers talking to us:

● Indignantly: "But that's not fair. You can't ground
me for just *one* D. Bob got a D when *he* was in 10th grade,
and you didn't do that to him."

● Frantically: "Where did you put my other
notebook?"

● Rebelliously: "Well, I can't help it. She didn't tell us
that assignment was going to be counted for our grade."

Speech is behavior. So are actions. We see things our
teenagers do—or fail to do:

● We see socks on the bedroom floor.

● During the worship service, we hear the flawless
and serene flute solo—after our daughter has agonized over
it for weeks.

● We see him racing down the driveway to meet the
school bus, leaving his math book and half-completed
homework lying forlornly by the door.

● We hear the screen door, the front door and the
bedroom door slam in rapid sequence, telling us that school
didn't go well today.

Behavior is what we see and hear. Usually we respond
to our teenagers' behaviors with behaviors of our own. We
approve or don't approve. We encourage some behaviors
and try to prevent others. We want to correct a tendency to
forget school assignments, so we lecture, threaten, punish
or remind (nag). We want the report card to return to its

former level, so we lay down new homework rules.

It's been that way all along. When Gina grabbed a forbidden cookie as a toddler, her mother frowned and said, "No, no!" When her brother splashed his way home from first grade one day through all the rain puddles he could find, his parents responded with behaviors—severe words, a spanking and half an hour of solitude in his bedroom.

Meeting behavior with behavior is a pattern parents are used to. Many will continue this pattern for the rest of their lives. Generation after generation, many people are aware of and deal with only one level of reality—the one visible on the surface.

But it's not the only level where we can deal with other human beings. There are other, deeper levels where we can observe our teenagers, approach them and, perhaps, even meet and influence them.

*M*otivations—Wants and Worries

Some people say that unless something motivates us, we would do absolutely nothing—never move, never speak, never think. They may be right. Unless we have some desire or feel some obligation to greet someone who enters the room, we don't look up, smile or speak. Unless we wonder—even vaguely—about what's on the radio or television, we don't turn it on. Unless we're hungry or curious or trying to accomplish something, we don't go into the kitchen and take inventory of the refrigerator's contents.

Motivations are the immediate, day-to-day impetus behind everything we do. The wants represent the carrot—what's out there ahead that we hope to have, what pulls us. The worries represent the stick—what we fear may happen, what pushes us. In other words, our behavior involves moving toward life's carrots and away from its sticks—toward the wants and away from the worries.

If Dan has the capacity to get A's and likes getting them, he'll do whatever he needs to do to get them. And if Dan doesn't care about A's himself but is afraid of the penalties (either practical or psychological) for *not* getting A's, he'll do whatever he thinks he must to get them. The observable results may be the same, but the two different motivations are quite different, and understanding these motivations will someday become important, either to Dan or his parents.

In a Search Institute study of 8,000 teenagers, the young people were asked how much they worry about 20 different things. Calculations placed the 20 issues in sequence from greatest to least importance to these teenagers. Understanding what teenagers worry about gives us some important clues to behaviors that would otherwise be irritating or puzzling. Here are the worries in the order the teenagers said they were troubled by them:[1]

I worry . . .

1. About how I'm doing in school.
2. About my looks.
3. About how well other kids like me.
4. That one of my parents might die.
5. About how my friends treat me.
6. About all the people who are hungry and poor in our country.
7. About all the violence that happens in our country.
8. That I might lose my best friend.
9. About all the drugs and drinking I see around me.
10. That I might not be able to get a good job when I'm older.
11. About whether my body is developing in a normal way.
12. That a nuclear bomb might be dropped on the United States.
13. That my parents might get a divorce.
14. That I may die soon.
15. That someone might force me to do sexual things I don't want to do.
16. That my friends will get me in trouble.
17. About how much my mother or father drinks.
18. That I might get beat up at school.

19. That one of my parents will hit me so hard that I will be badly hurt.

20. That I might kill myself.

Seeing worry about school at the head of the list won't surprise the many parents who see their teenagers living a pattern of disciplined attention to the requirements of learning. These parents can see the appropriate behaviors— talk and action demonstrated in regular home study, attention to homework deadlines, and conversations about assignments, tests and other academic concerns.

But when parents don't see that kind of behavior, one of two things is true: (a) their teenager's priorities aren't arranged in exactly this order; or (b) their teenager worries about school performance but isn't acting on that concern. And if a teenager isn't acting on an important concern, something else is probably getting in the way.

One issue that may be interfering with school performance is the fact that three of the next four items on the list involve social relationships. Concern about looking good, being liked by other kids or how other teenagers treat them may absorb so much time and activity that there's little left for school. That's Gina's situation.

Gina's parents might be able to respond more adequately if they understood Gina's behavior as something deeper than behavior but not so obvious. Adults tend to forget how important social relationships are to teenagers. If they understood this reality—whether or not anything about Gina changes—some of the puzzle about Gina's behavior and how she spends her time would dissipate. Moreover, if the parents expressed their understanding, their understanding might even cause some changes in Gina.

We know that when a worry or anxiety is never acknowledged or discussed in an understanding way, it often continues to produce puzzling behavior. But if the worry is acknowledged and talked about with a patient and understanding person (not teased about or labeled as wrong), the anxiety level falls.

Researchers have discovered, for example, that teenagers who worry about nuclear war but can express that worry by talking about it are better adjusted than teenagers who don't acknowledge their concern.[2] To some degree, talking about the things that worry us actually lessens the worry's intensity.

One day Jody came home complaining that her art teacher was being unfair by not accepting a late drawing. When Jody's mother asked, "But didn't I see it practically finished last week?" Jody shamefacedly dragged the picture out from under her bed. After a moment of painful silence she said: "It's really so awful. And I knew Mrs. Harris would think it was terrible, so I just didn't hand it in. I wanted to hand it in, but Mrs. Harris says she thinks I have real talent, and I just couldn't let her see this!"

When Jody's mother saw the two conflicting motivations Jody was struggling with, she could respond with understanding and compassion rather than a lecture about uncompleted work. Jody had made her decision and was having to live with the outcome. What she needed from her mother was not judgment but a supportive hug and an encouraging, "I know how hard it is to make decisions like that."

Gina's parents could learn from Jody's mother. Instead of lecturing Gina about what she's *not* doing, it would be more helpful for her parents to talk to her about what she *is* doing. Gina is more likely to hear and care about what her parents hope for her if they first acknowledge what's important to her.

It would feel good to Gina if one of her parents someday said something such as: "Your looks are pretty important nowadays, aren't they? I understand how it is. You want others to think you look nice; you want them to be your friends. I remember how important that was to me too."

Virtually everything your teenager does has its roots somewhere in a motivation of some kind. Knowing what's going on at that level can do several things, one of which is to make more sense of what your teenager does, leading you to greater understanding. And after understanding may come insight.

In addressing your teenager's attitudes toward school and learning, try meeting him or her at the level of motivations. Talk about what you guess concerns him or her. Motivations have their greatest power when they remain unacknowledged, unmentioned, unchallenged. If Gina's behavior is to change, someone will have to meet her at the level of motivation. Otherwise, we'll all have to wait to see whether her motivations mature as she matures.

🍎 Values—What's Important in Life

Beneath behavior and motivations is another, deeper level of reality. It's composed of the things that have long-term value—the things that, in our serious moments, form for us life's goals and purposes.

Purposes, goals and values aren't the exclusive property of adults. Teenagers have them too—even if few of the adults in their lives recognize the values. The same Search Institute survey that produced the hierarchy of worries also produced a ranking of values. Although some of the same items appear on this list, they appear in different places. The difference doesn't represent an inaccuracy, inconsistency or something that's true only of teenagers.

Whether we are teenagers or adults, our long-range plans and hopes are often different from the things that absorb our attention from moment to moment. The motivations are moment-to-moment; values are long-range. Anyone who has ever broken a fingernail or had a slight crick in the neck knows that momentary concerns can capture attention far out of proportion to their importance in the general scheme of things.

To get different answers you must ask different questions. The survey question that introduced the worries list was, "How much do you worry . . . ?" The question that introduced the values list was, "How important in life is it to you . . . ?" These 8,000 teenagers ranked their values in the following order from highest to lowest:[3]

1. To have a happy family life.
2. To get a good job when I am older.
3. To do something important with my life.
4. To do well in school.
5. To make my parents proud of me.
6. To have a world without war.
7. To have friends I can count on.
8. To feel good about myself.
9. To have God at the center of my life.
10. To have lots of fun and good times.
11. To have a world without hunger and poverty.
12. To feel safe and secure in my neighborhood.
13. To understand my feelings.
14. To make my own decisions.
15. To be part of a church.
16. To do things that help people.
17. To be really good at sports.
18. To have clothes and hair that look good to other kids.
19. To have things (such as clothes, records, etc.) as nice as other kids have.
20. To be popular at school.
21. To have lots of money.
22. To be different in some way from all the other kids I know.
23. To do whatever I want to do, when I want to do it.
24. To be good in music, drama or art.

Teenagers know school performance has considerable long-range importance. Only three goals—having a happy family life, having a good job in maturity and doing something important with life—precede it.

On the worries list, looking good to others and being popular rank high. However, when you ask about long-term importance, you get a completely different set of priorities. Most adults are surprised to see how low the popularity and materialistic values rank on this list.

To know our teenagers as well as they can be known, we must go deeper than what motivates their day-to-day behavior and ask what's important to them in life. The joking question, "Will it matter 100 years from now?" isn't often helpful when your teenager is smarting from a disastrous test grade. But it illustrates a step in the right direction—a step toward perspective and value. What *is* important, long-term?

Nowadays, Rory practices law. Twenty years ago, he was a ninth-grade problem. Every school staff member knew him well. They knew his mother too. She was often summoned for consultation. Rory's report cards covered the range from A's to D's. He came often to the counselor's office—and even more often warmed the mourners bench outside the principal's office.

The "bad" behavior of this reasonable, intelligent, caring 14-year-old made sense only when approached at the level of his values. Otherwise, he was an enigma. He had an intense commitment to learning; yet he almost failed English. He could complete most math assignments in half the time it took other students; yet he sometimes failed to submit his homework.

Rory marched to the beat of a different drummer. The third value on the list had taken hold of him, powerfully influencing both his motivations and behaviors. Rory wanted to do something important with his life, and he didn't consider the age of 14 too early to start.

Rory had grasped that one way to influence the shape of the world was through its political life, and he was eager to learn. Four years before he could vote, he was distributing literature outside political caucus rooms and wangling his way into his party's district convention.

On weekends the committed teenager often distributed literature in shopping malls or trudged from door to door asking for signatures on a petition. Of course, this work meant some sacrifice of time for his social studies class. He didn't always completely answer his questions about the agricultural productivity of Afghanistan.

"Ralph, I appreciate your interest in surgical procedures. But practicing emergency appendectomies is beyond the scope of high school biology."

He almost failed English entirely. When a young man is devoted to changing the world, the nuts and bolts of ninth-grade English sometimes chafe. He *knew* how to spell the spelling words, and he resented the 20 minutes the teacher scheduled to allow him—and everyone else in class—to prove it.

Then when the class studied *Evangeline*, he wanted to dig deeper into the sociological factors underlying the transplantation of the Canadian immigrants to the southern United States than his teacher would allow. And because of his persistence, Rory was eventually ejected from the classroom.

Give Rory credit for passionately wanting to know more about a subject he cared about. Give the principal credit for taking the passion seriously and spending 20 minutes discussing Rory's question (while the office secretary no doubt wondered at the length of the disciplinary procedure taking place).

"I know I must make Mrs. Cooper miserable some-times," Rory explained. "But I get so *interested* in why things happen the way they do, and I want to talk about them."

Our values influence us—sometimes even at the cost of pain to ourselves and others.

It's sad to note that something as powerful as life-values are so seldom discussed among parents and children. Even though your teenager may not be another Rory, a talk with him or her about goals and purpose may present you with some pleasant surprises—a discovery, perhaps, that your teenager thinks about much more significant matters than you knew. Talking about these deeper levels of reality will bring you to greater understanding.

Spiritual Identity—Our Place in the Universe

We can meet and understand our teenagers at a level that's even deeper than long-range goals and values. It's the level of our spiritual identity—who we are in the family, in our community of friends or co-workers, in relationship to the world and in relationship to God. Some people pass through life without ever asking questions about life's meaning or what difference it makes what we do or believe. The result is meaninglessness and despair. Out of that void arise behaviors such as a single-minded devotion to collecting adult toys or a frantic pursuit of the symbols of worth and success—like children who relentlessly strive for top grades.

You can trace the power of our spiritual identity up through all the other levels of reality. It affects our choice of values, our wants and worries, and our behavior.

"I don't know whether you know Anne Munson or not," Mrs. Snyder said as she sat down in the counselor's office. The counselor nodded, recognizing the name. "She's in my third hour social studies class. She's a nice girl, and I think she's quite bright. But it's like pulling teeth to get her to say anything. When I call on her, she usually smiles at me and shakes her head. It isn't that she doesn't know the answer—what she writes shows she does understand. It's more like she's saying, 'I don't want to talk right now.'

"Once or twice, when I've persisted, she has answered. But her voice is so soft I have to stand right beside her to hear. I don't know whether you can tell me or not, but I just wonder if there's something I ought to know about her."

There is. Anne is an only child who lives on a truck farm with her parents. Because she had no other children to play with as a child, her parents were her only society. Her parents attended church with strict regularity, and they reared Anne the same way—strictly.

Anne believes in a God much like the one her parents believe in. God—who knows everything and who is everywhere—watches over her. She supposes that God watches over her partly to protect her but also, she senses, to check up on what she's doing, saying and thinking, lest she "fall into sin." However, she doesn't really know what falling into sin entails, since her parents have often harshly pun-

ished her for something that was, to her, quite innocent—
reading something or saying something they considered
sinful.

Because of this background, Anne sees herself as a tiny,
insignificant being in a universe controlled by a Transcendent Watcher. One of her central values is survival. What she
worries about most is incurring the disapproval of this
powerful being—who she's not really sure is friend or
enemy. And what she wants most is not to attract anyone's
attention.

When we understand the kind of universe Anne lives in
and the kind of God she believes controls it, it's easy to
understand the values and worries that cause her behaviors—her extreme shyness, her reluctance to speak and
her desperate attempt to hide, even from those who only
want to help her.

Our spiritual identity strikes at the heart of who we
are and how we perceive ourselves. Out of it grows our
sense of self-esteem and self-worth. If our teenagers see
themselves as valuable parts of God's universe and our
families, their values, motivations and behaviors are likely
to be positive and self-affirming. But if they see themselves
as insignificant or unwanted, their values and motivations
will likely result, long-term, in negative or self-destructive
behaviors.

Few parents ever address these issues with their
teenagers. It's quite probable that Gina has never heard her
parents talk about lifetime goals or values. And it's even
more likely that she has never heard them mention spiritual
identity—either their own or Gina's. Less than a third of
10- to 15-year-olds say their families ever talk at home
about God or other religious things.[4] The percentage is
probably even smaller of those who talk about the overall
purpose of human life—or their own lives in particular.
And how many discuss whether the universe is friendly,
unfriendly or merely aimless?

Meeting your teenager at the level of spiritual identity
means, at the very least, that questions about the origin

and meanings of life can be asked aloud in your home. It also means that you sometimes, in your teenager's hearing, ask those questions yourself.

When we ask these questions aloud, we make an important statement. We say that these questions are worth asking—that they are important. We also acknowledge that there are some important ways in which we all are alike. Whether we're children, teenagers, elders, educated or uneducated, there's a great deal we don't know. We ask questions, and we try to push back the veil of mystery. In the process of asking, we discover or remember those stories of the Christian faith, those hints of joy in our personal history and in our experience of faith that remind us that we're held in honor and care by a loving God.

As Paul pointed out in 1 Timothy 4:8, we teach our children to prepare for a longer future than we tend to think about most of the time. Our children's future extends into eternity. Knowing that, we do well to make nurturing their consciousness of their spiritual identity a central element of their education.

One of the greatest gifts we can give our children is a view of life and of themselves that consciously concentrates more attention on the deeper levels. And as we try to turn our children's attention to their own motivations, values and spiritual identity, we often discover that we're giving more attention to all of these matters in our own lives as well.

 CHAPTER 4

When the Report Card Comes Home

Issuing and receiving report cards is an important ritual in the education process. Everyone knows it. Though teenagers may publicly deny the report card's importance (it isn't cool to appear to care much about grades), they know grades matter.

Report cards are visible evidence of "how I'm doing." Teenagers *want* the visible evidence that they're doing well. They also know that good grades are important to their parents. As a result, the anxiety level in the classrooms and corridors rises sharply when the time comes to distribute report cards.

Most parents simply don't know how profoundly their attitudes and unguarded comments about grades affect not only their children's attitudes toward education but their chances for academic success. When they bring home their report cards, teenagers are vulnerable. Unless the card is top-notch, containing a set of grades that's absolutely everything both they and their parents hope for, they can be easily hurt.

As a parent, you are an important "beholder" to your teenager. Don't even try to hide that importance. How you react to your teenager's report card is highly significant.

Teenagers know their parents sometimes attach different meanings to grades than they themselves do. Receiving a C in music appreciation may satisfy Ben, who has no enthusiasm for "all that old-fashioned stuff." But his mother, who once taught piano, wants to see something better than a C in any music course Ben takes.

Since you are such an important audience for your teenager's grades, let's look at what you do when the grades are brought home. What, exactly, happens? Read the following questions, noting the answers. Each question may sound insignificant—scarcely worth asking. But, taken together, they're more meaningful than they sound.

1. If you are home when your teenager arrives with a report card, do you look at it immediately? ☐ Yes ☐ No

2. Do you ask your teenager to stay with you while you look at the report card? ☐ Yes ☐ No

3. If you find the report card when your teenager isn't present, do you look at it then, or do you wait for your first look when your teenager is present? ☐ Look ☐ Wait

4. After reading the grades, do you return the report card with or without comment? ☐ With ☐ Without

5. If there has been either a positive or negative change in grades, do you comment on the change? ☐ Yes ☐ No

6. If there have been changes in both directions, which direction do you comment on first? ☐ Positive ☐ Negative

7. Do you thank your teenager for showing you the report card? ☐ Yes ☐ No

The small, seemingly insignificant details of things we do and say, and the sequence in which we do and say them, reveal a lot about our attitudes and assumptions as parents. And these apparently trivial actions, repeated day after day, year after year, cause our children to know us much more thoroughly than we might guess.

Whether you're aware of it or not, you give three messages when your teenager's grades come home— messages disclosed in your answers to those seven questions. The messages are about ownership, appreciation and support, and they strongly influence your teenager's feelings about school. When those feelings about school become evident to you sometime in the future, you'll probably have no idea that you had anything to do with them. But you did.

When school grades come home, the three things you can do that will most help your teenager are:

1. Demonstrate that you believe the grades are your teenager's, not your own.

2. React appreciatively to whatever you can honestly applaud.

3. After that, offer your support—your interest, your caring, your love, and your encouragement of your teenager's efforts to get a good education.

Ownership

The first issue defined when your teenager brings home grades is their *ownership*. Whose grades are they— your teenager's or yours? A teenager has rights to his or her own improved grades and motivation to learn. However closely you were involved, however enthusiastically you were cheering (or prodding) on the sidelines, it was your teenager who went to class, joined in the discussions, completed the homework and took the tests. They're your teenager's grades, and you make it clear whether or not you believe that in several ways.

Jean's mother wasn't at home when she arrived with her report card. Jean was feeling wonderful. She had managed a C in history, after three straight D's. And she had moved up from C to C+ in two other classes. She was watching television when her mother arrived. At the end of the show, she switched off the television and went to her mom's bedroom where her mother was changing out of her office clothes.

"Did you see my grades?" Jean inquired eagerly.

From inside the dress her mother was pulling over her head came a muffled, "Mm, I did."

"Did you like them?"

"Yes," said her mother, now in the clear and reaching for her jeans. "They look pretty good."

Feeling the need for another look at the happy evidence and a little more celebration, Jean ran to the kitchen counter where she had laid the envelope. It wasn't there. Hurrying back to the bedroom, her brow furrowed, Jean asked, "Where is it? Where did you put my report card?"

"Oh, I put it away in the file drawer where I keep things like that. You can get it out again if you want."

Without knowing it, Jean's mother sent a clear message to Jean: Your grades belong to me. In response to that message, Jean's attitude toward schoolwork changes slightly. In some small way, her motivation is reduced and she cares a little less about doing well in school. After all, is it worth all the extra effort if she works hard to improve her grades only for her mother's benefit?

If you are home when your teenager arrives with a report card, do you look at it immediately? If you find the report card when your teenager isn't present, do you look at it then, or do you wait for your first look when your teenager is present? Do you thank your teenager for showing you his or her report card?

These questions indicate the signals you send your teenager about ownership. Looking at a report card the moment it arrives shows the courtesy you'd extend to an adult friend who wants to show you something important. On the other hand, if the grades are yours, you can choose your own time to examine them.

If you're at home when your teenager arrives with a

report card in hand, that's an event. It happens no more than four to six times a year. Stop whatever else you're doing and look. Look at the grades together with your teenager, and hand them back to the teenager when you finish. Say, "Thanks for showing them to me, Son." Expressing thanks for the conversation is another way to demonstrate your belief that the grades are the teenager's, not yours.

Jean's mother wasn't home when Jean arrived. When her mother did come home, she saw the envelope, opened it, viewed the contents and filed the report card away. If she really believed the grades were Jean's, she could have called Jean to see them with her right then, or she could have waited until Jean was available to look at them with her. She should then have asked if Jean wanted them filed or wanted to keep them herself—an owner's decision.

🍎 Appreciation

Do you ask your teenager to stay with you while you look at the report card? After reading the grades, do you return the report card with or without comment? If there has been either a positive or negative change in grades, do you comment on the change?

These questions indicate whether you express appreciation of your teenager's grades. Teenagers can't expect their friends to give them any pats on the back for better grades. Friends have their own grades to celebrate or worry about, and some of them may be competing with your teenager for scarce places on the "grading ladder." If anyone hears Jean's feelings about her grades and expresses appreciation of her work, it had better be her parents.

Expressing appreciation is important. After all, one time you discover that people love you is when they're as happy about good things happening to you as you are for yourself. Maybe that's what all teenagers are really listening for when they bring grades home: some evidence that their parents love them that much.

When you look at a report card together with your

teenager, not only can you show who owns the grades, but you can express your appreciation of them. "Hey, you went up in three subjects! Wonderful! What did you do to make that happen?" Since grades don't usually rise on their own, Jean must have been exercising a disciplined effort to do better. And she has succeeded. When you succeed, one of the things you need most is an appreciative person to affirm your success.

If there have been changes in both directions, which direction do you comment on first?

It's not realistic to assume that every grade your teenager brings home will represent improvement. Grades go down as well as up. But first comment favorably on whatever you can find to appreciate—even if it's no more than, "Good! You kept your grade in English where it was the last time, and I know that's hard for you." Then the stage will be better set for a useful and supportive conversation about the bad news.

🍎 Support

More than anything else, teenagers need supportive conversation—particularly at report-card time. "Supportive" combines in a single word such wonderful concepts as caring, concern, understanding and encouragement.

If the grades have gone down, most teenagers don't need a stern lecture but a warm hug, followed by a supportive message. An appropriate message says something such as: "We're still your parents. We love and value you. Part of that loving is expecting you to do as well as you can in school. We want to do whatever we can, within reason, to help you do that."

If a D has appeared where there used to be a C, why not begin with some questions such as these?

● "How do you feel about that grade?"

● "Do you want to do something about it next term?"

● "Given the material and the class you're in, do you think it's possible for you to change your grade? Or is this about what you can expect?''

Remember, it's your teenager's grade.

Parents Who Discourage

Not every teenager receives a positive and healthy re-action to a report card at home. Many parents underreact, overreact or react negatively. Each response hurts the teenager and the teenager's view of education.

Saying too little. Some report cards go home to parents who show little interest. They glance at the grades but make no comment. These parents convey the message that education isn't important, and that what their teenager does in school doesn't particularly interest them.

But—most destructive of all—they also communicate that their teenager isn't worth much of their time or concern.

The best hope for these teenagers is that they have another adult in their lives—perhaps a teacher, a youth minister, or a friend's parent—who does care about them, who will listen, celebrate their good news and soothe the sting of their losses.

Saying too much. At the other extreme from parents who say nothing are the parents who say too much. That was the case with the Beckwiths.

Randy knew there would be the usual lecture when he showed his report card, so he always delayed the news as long as possible. He said nothing about his grades when they were issued in March, hoping his parents would forget to call the office. But they didn't.

''When do report cards come out?'' his mother asked the principal's secretary.

''Oh, didn't Randy get his report card? They came out two weeks ago last Friday. I'll mail you a duplicate.''

Randy was good at inventing explanations for his laxity. He had already used ''I lost it in my locker'' last marking period and ''I put it in my science book, but now it's not there'' the one before. ''Maybe I was absent that day," he offered, lamely.

"We'll get it in the mail," his mother tersely responded. "Just you wait."

Randy knew his parents would be upset, and he knew why. The grades were not good, and the report card's comment section was sure to contain notes such as "homework missing," "lacks effort" and "missing makeup work."

As soon as he walked in the door the next day after school, he knew the report card had arrived. "Come in here. I want you to explain this thing to me," his father growled. "What do you mean, getting a report card like this?"

His mother wasn't much better. She didn't yell; she whined. "What's going to happen to you, Randy? You'll never even graduate if you keep on like this. How are you going to get a job if you don't graduate?"

Randy's parents had a lot to say. Randy mostly listened. They told him he'd have to shape up or they'd ground him. They'd reduce his allowance if he got the same grades next time. And so on, and so on. It wasn't much fun, but it eventually ended. Randy could get out of the house for a while to let them cool off.

What saved Randy from complete despair was that the lectures and the threats were much like the ones he'd heard the last time and the time before that. He knew that his parents would pretty much ignore his schooling until the next report card came out—when he'd hear it all again.

These parents convey a confusing message. On one hand, the parents appear to attach great importance to grades. But on the other hand, school doesn't appear to matter at all. As a result, the teenager is either confused or growing increasingly cynical about both parents and education. Randy's grades probably won't change much in the near future, nor will the school performance they represent.

Saying the wrong things. Some parents do and say discouraging things under the mistaken notion that they're helping their teenager. These parents genuinely care about their teenager's school experience and consider themselves helpful and positive. Having heard that high expectations contribute to greater academic achievement (as indeed they do, when appropriately expressed), these parents set the bar of expectations just slightly higher than whatever level the student has achieved.

Parents such as these appear never to be entirely pleased. Teachers' comments may include, "shows good effort," "enthusiastic," "uses study time well." But the parent raises the bar a notch: "Anybody should be able to get B's if they try hard enough"; or "There's no reason in the world why those two B+'s couldn't be A's."

Too many parents play this switch-up game. In fact, there is a clear difference between the quality of work and test results necessary for a B+ and an A. Pretending there's no difference is unfair to the teenager.

Another kind of parent plays the switch-down game: "As far as I'm concerned, a D is no better than an F." This game can be tailored to fit any spot on the grade scale: B's are the same as C's, C's are the same as D's, and so on. It's a discouraging way to talk about school performance, and it often has the opposite of the intended effect. Unfortunately, most parents don't realize the pressure these games exert and how hopeless they make their teenager feel.

🍎 *Better Ways to Respond*

How can parents be supportive, helpful, corrective, encouraging, reassuring and affirming of their teenager at report-card time? When the grades are high and the comments positive, it's not much of a problem. But what about when the opposite is true?

Don't rush. First of all, don't rush into anything. Take your time. No quick reactions. No furrowed brow. Unless you're among the few parents who see a report card that's exactly as you hoped it would be, thank your teenager for showing it to you and suggest that you talk about it at a less hectic time (unless, of course, you first see it at a non-

"Okay, everyone! It's time to talk
about Mary's report card."

hectic time and have the leisure to talk then).

Keep it private. Don't make the discussion of the report card a family event. Having more than one child present raises the likelihood of drawing damaging comparisons ("*I* didn't get any D's at all and you've got two!"), and it provides fertile material for siblings to use later to needle each other.

Focus on motivations and values. Questions that begin with "why" aren't much use when discussing falling grades. "Why did you go down in English?" The answer invariably is either "I don't know" or a string of observable facts—"I did this and the teacher did (or didn't do) that." Behavior. Surface stuff. Instead, try moving down to the level of motivations. "Did you worry about your grade in English? Were you afraid of getting this kind of grade?"

A good question with any kind of report card is, "How do you feel about your grades this time?" Such a question takes your conversation beneath the surface level to feelings and worries. It also puts the teenager in center stage, where the emphasis belongs.

Once again, no matter how deeply you may feel about the reported grades, they aren't yours. If change is to occur, it's your teenager who will have to do most of the changing. And the changing, if it comes, will occur at the level of motivations or values. When those change, the behavior will change by itself.

Be patient. Your teenager probably feels much the same as you do about the grades, and will say so. However, if you and your teenager aren't accustomed to a conversational style that's both serious and mutually respectful, the teenager's first response to your inquiries about grades is likely to be a muttered, "I don't know."

Try again. Start asking about the individual subjects. What went into the figuring of the grade? What kinds of classroom activities did the class do in the past term? Is the grade a surprise? And, again, if you haven't received a direct expression, ask, "How do you feel about your grade in that class?" Another good question at the same deeper level is, "What would you like to make happen in this course during the next marking period?"

Watch your tone. A lot of whether your teenager feels your support depends on your tone of voice and facial expression when asking questions about the report card.

If your teenager senses that the questions are real, asked with respect and interest, and not the kickoff of a lecture, you're likely to get a straight and informative answer. If the grades are disappointing, the teenager most fears an emotional outburst accompanied by a lengthy, sermonizing lecture. When you don't react that way and when your teenager is reassured that you're on his or her team, you can work together on some real planning to correct the situation.

Adjust expectations if necessary. Most students want to answer honestly about their grades—unless they're afraid of your reaction. Perhaps your teenager says: "I think that's about all I can expect in that class. I just don't like the subject, and it's hard." Such a response tells you a lot. If you also find out that your teenager has been responsible with homework and assignments, then your teenager's statement about the current grade may be accurate. It doesn't matter whether you liked biology; if the teenager doesn't, and everything connected with the class is a chore, you probably need to readjust your expectations. Otherwise, be prepared for continued pain and conflict.

Treat your teenager with respect. Often, when the emotional weather is fair and mild, students express disappointment with themselves and talk about their determination to do better next term. Such a declaration from your teenager, giving evidence of internal motivation, is infinitely superior to imposing your own will, restrictions and goals on him or her.

A parent must become skilled at discerning the difference between answers "just to please" and answers of genuine intent. No matter which you think it is, move the discussion to ways in which the positive change can occur.

Now's the time to talk about behavior—maybe your

own, maybe your teenager's. How can you help? Does your teenager need a change of home routine to allow for some (or more) scheduled study time? Does he or she need an early ride to school to get extra help from a teacher? Could he or she use better access to library references? When the student sees you as part of his or her team, not an adversary, the door to improvement begins to swing open.

Parents who've tried dealing with their teenager more respectfully have often been pleasantly surprised. Respect begets respect. However, if you like the idea but, when you try it, find yourself slipping back into old, well-practiced parenting patterns, the change may be too difficult to manage without coaching. Look for a school or family counselor who can help you develop new relationship patterns to help you and your teenager through a difficult but potentially hopeful and relationship-healing time.

CHAPTER 5

What Grades Can You Expect?

As a parent, you want the best for your teenager. You know grades are important for college and career. And you want your teenager to excel—for his or her own sake.

But in your desire for your child to have the best in life, do you sometimes expect better grades than you should from your teenager? Can all teenagers always get A's? Does a young person have to excel in every subject? Two common reactions we have to teenagers' grades uncover our hidden expectations. They also help us discover what grades we can reasonably expect from our teenagers. Let's look at these reactions as well as some factors that influence our teenagers' grades.

"... But She Could Do Better"

What's a reasonable grade for your teenager? That's really the crucial question when you consider what grades to expect. We wish we could count how many parent-teacher conferences we sat through in which teachers, principals or counselors invariably concluded their comments with, ". . . but she could do better."

Of course, they're right. Couldn't we all do better? We could all find ways to improve whatever we do. There's always a way to be a more perfect parent, a better hedge trimmer, a better counselor, a better manager, a more skilled cook. However, we need to ask ourselves some tough questions before we insist that our teenagers always do "better" in school. Does being better at any particular skill or pursuit define our importance in the world's eyes? in God's eyes? And if we're not willing to be urged toward greater excellence in our own endeavors, is it fair to urge it onto our teenagers? Probably not. When is a student's present level of effort and achievement "good enough"?

It's wonderful when parents ask, "What is a *reasonable* grade for my teenager?" The question makes eminently good sense. It makes as much sense as the kinds of questions we ask ourselves: "What is a reasonable meal I can prepare after eight hours on the job?" Or "What is the reasonable amount of hacking at the hedge to keep it from taking over the yard?" We set limits on our efforts on any job to keep from being reduced to helplessness by attempting perfection on everything we touch. Our teenagers deserve the same consideration.

What can I reasonably expect of my teenager in junior or senior high school? To answer such a question fairly, you need to consider numerous factors—effort, interest, handicaps, peer competition, course difficulty, educational and cultural background, and motivation. By working through these factors with a teacher or counselor, together you can come to a tentative agreement about reasonable expectations.

In some ways, educators have an advantage over parents in assessing what's realistic for a particular teenager. They know certain things about your teenager from other teachers' reports, from observations, and from tested abilities and skills. They can compare your teenager's performance with his or her classmates' work. And they know whether your child is making a reasonable effort, keeping current on assignments, listening alertly in class, keeping material organized and contributing to classroom discussion.

If these ingredients are in place and the grade is still a D, perhaps that course, that type of study, or that activity is not where the student's major talents lie. In this case, it may be unreasonable to expect more from your teenager.

Like everyone else, students need to know that what they've done is reasonable—good enough. To be told constantly that they're short of the mark never motivates. Instead, it drives them toward frustration and despair, and they begin telling themselves that there's no use trying. We dare not push any human being to that point—certainly not the young person we're trying to bring through a time already fraught with new challenges.

"If He'd Only Try Harder . . ."

Too many parents genuinely believe effort is the only ingredient in getting good grades. But only in mythical Lake Wobegon are all the children above average. In real schools with competitive grading systems, many students will earn below-average grades (C- or below).

If your teenager receives below-average grades in some classes, accept it. Leaning on him or her to do better while ignoring limitations of ability, interest or skill won't change reality. In fact, such an approach will likely make your teenager feel even less enthusiastic about learning. And it could drive the two of you apart.

We all have our strengths and weaknesses, and we're not all equally good at everything. Sara, for example, excelled at physical activity. She drew straight A's in physical education classes. She participated in varsity sports and was an asset to any team she played on.

But academic subjects were a struggle. Her grades hovered between C's and D's. After a rocky year with 10th-grade biology, Sara decided not to try chemistry and physics. Instead, she took a semester each of astronomy and oceanography, finding them both interesting and pleasant. She limited her math to elementary algebra, plane geometry and some computer programming.

Sara's below-average grades weren't the result of little effort or poor organization. She made reasonable effort, got her assignments in on time, and—except for straight A's in physical education—achieved C's and D's in most of her courses. There was no reason to get upset with Sara. The grades she received accurately reflected her own gifts and abilities.

Jason was just the opposite. In the gym he had two left feet, couldn't hit a basket, and was generally clumsy. Woodworking class—which he decided to try "so I can make something neat for my parents"—was equally unrewarding. Only a mother as loving as his would have displayed the spice rack her son produced! But Jason breezed through trigonometry and calculus, loved college preparatory English, and conducted abstruse experiments in the physics lab.

These stories illustrate the truth of 1 Corinthians 12:4a: "There are different kinds of gifts . . ."

 ## Making Choices

Grades are sometimes a reward, sometimes a punishment. They can be a prize or a pronouncement of failure. And they don't always seem fair. To achieve a given grade in calculus, one student may have invested many hours of determined slogging, resolutely ignoring the shouts of friends who are celebrating spring, the delights of being young and having a Frisbee. Yet another student may have made the same grade without any sacrifice, having inherited a mind that embraces mathematical concepts with relish.

A given grade does not always carry the same message. Like art, grades achieve meaning chiefly in the eye of the beholder. While a B in French may represent victory for one student, it means failure for another.

Given that each student is different, should a teenager avoid those classes in which they know, from the start, they won't be able to get high grades? Sometimes yes, sometimes no. On one hand, there's no sense in your teenager taking a difficult course he or she will neither enjoy nor need. But on the other hand, exposure to classes in unfamiliar fields expands a student's understanding and can be of great value—as long as the grade isn't the central focus.

After our younger daughter had plowed through a challenging load of academic courses as a high school sophomore and junior, she decided intentionally to broaden her experience in her senior year. She dropped out of the accelerated math track and, in its place, registered for an art course. "I don't know anything about art," she said, "and I'll probably drive the teacher crazy. But I want to know what art buffs learn. I have enough credits to graduate without this one, so I'll take the class without credit and enjoy myself."

That's what she did. She also tried out for the school musical and the spring drama. She didn't astonish the director with her talent, but she worked backstage in one production, landed a bit part in the end-of-the-year musical and, in the process, acquired a working knowledge of play production. The less demanding academic schedule also left her enough after-school time to join a madrigal group.

Now our daughter is a pastor. Who is to say she would be better off if she had stuck with her more demanding courses? Is she more likely someday to need to know how to direct a drama or to solve a calculus problem?

Every teenager is wonderfully unique. It's important for all of them to strike a balance between perfecting their own particular strengths and exploring the rest of the academic world. Parents can help their teenagers think through the decisions and search for the balance between perfecting and exploring. But remember: The final decision should almost always belong to the teenager.

Getting Along With Legendary Mr. Grim

Throughout this chapter we've talked about characteristics of students that influence grades. We also need to remember another human factor in the grade equation: teachers.

"What's so funny, anyway?"

Teachers can be powerful motivators for their students. As adults, we can recall those teachers in elementary and secondary school whose energy, knowledge or personal concern left an indelible mark on our life and career.

Yet we also remember the "other" teachers. Rarely does a teenager get through secondary school without running into a Mr. Grim. Mr. Grim has many manifestations:

● Some Grims are classroom tyrants—holdovers from the days of corporal punishment for classroom offenses.

● Others have no sense of humor—a dreadful calamity to energetic teenagers.

● Some haven't rewritten a lesson plan nor a test in years. "If it isn't broke, why fix it?"

● And some are simply boring. You saw it yourself at parents night when half the parents nodded off during one 12-minute session.

We'd rather not talk about teachers—any teachers—in less than positive terms, because we speak about our friends. But, we must confess, the quality of teachers varies. Teaching has many dimensions, and some teachers fail to rank high on any of them. They get by, and the students they teach get by. Of course, thoroughly motivated students can learn even without the help of inspired teaching. But it's much harder.

How can you help a teenager who comes home declaring that he or she has had it with Mr. Grim? Your first step should be to consult the school administration. Without drawing conclusions or making accusations, report what you've heard. Most administrators appreciate parents who report, factually and briefly, what they've heard is going on at school and then ask for clarification. Sometimes you'll hear another side to the story that also makes sense. Or you'll discover that the school is already working to correct a difficult situation.

But let's suppose you've checked it out and there's nothing the administration can do about a particular teacher problem. Every administrator would like every student to have a perfect teacher. But administrators have to make do with imperfect teachers—just as teenagers have to make do with imperfect parents.

What can you do? You've suggested getting another teacher, but that door is closed. And your teenager has to stay in the class because it's a required course. You realize that your teenager will just have to get through the year. It won't be fun, but it has to be done. What then?

It is your teenager, not you, who has to go into the classroom every day. Your teenager, not you, has to listen to the class proceedings, answer the questions posed, do the assignments, take the tests. Thus your teenager, not you, has to develop a method to deal with Mr. Grim on his or her own. (At least there's a positive benefit to the problem: Difficult people will always be part of your teenager's life. Learning to deal with a difficult person in authority can be a valuable education in itself.)

Like other people, teachers live on several levels of reality. You and your teenager see the boring or dull or cranky or too-firm behavior. But there's more to Mr. Grim than behavior. He has wants and worries. Beneath them are values—some sense of what's important in life. If you and your teenager begin to meet Mr. Grim at one of these other levels, it could change things.

One way to start dealing with Mr. Grim would be to ask your teenager (not you) to answer and think about the following kinds of questions:

1. Do you know why Mr. Grim first ☐ Yes ☐ No
decided to become a teacher?

2. Do you know what other careers ☐ Yes ☐ No
Mr. Grim considered before deciding to
teach?

3. In the past month, have you tried to ☐ Yes ☐ No
start a one-to-one conversation with Mr.
Grim before class, after class, in the hall, at
a basketball game?

4. Do you know whether Mr. Grim has ☐ Yes ☐ No
any children? any pets? Where does he shop
for groceries? What library does he use?

5. Do you know what he likes to do in   ☐ Yes ☐ No
his spare time?

6. In the past month have you offered   ☐ Yes ☐ No
a positive comment to him?

7. Teachers get lots of negative   ☐ Yes ☐ No
surprises—homework not done, lessons not
learned, practical jokes. Have you ever
prepared a positive surprise for your
teacher (an unexpected note on your hand-
in assignment, a cartoon you think will
tickle his funny bone)?

8. Does Mr. Grim know what you like   ☐ Yes ☐ No
best about his class?

Let's look at these questions and how they can help
your teenager cope with Mr. Grim. Again, encourage your
teenager to respond—instead of taking action for him or
her.

*Do you know why Mr. Grim first decided to become a
teacher? Do you know what other careers Mr. Grim considered before deciding to teach?* At some point in his life,
Mr. Grim chose to be a teacher. Other options were un-
doubtedly open to him when he was in college. But he
chose to teach. Something about teaching must have
attracted him—something he saw in it that pleased him.
Moreover, something about teaching must still attract him.
After all, he did sign a contract to teach this year.

People teach for lots of reasons. They like teenagers.
They like the subject matter. They like the long summer
vacations. Their reasons are nearly always positive. People
don't become teachers because there was nothing else to
do.

Your teenager can find out what attracts Mr. Grim to
teach. What pulls him toward teaching? What are the
goodies in it? By asking him in person, your teenager might
be doing him a favor. Maybe life has so obscured his original feelings about the teaching profession that he hasn't
thought about them for months.

When your teenager finds out why the teacher chose

to teach, he or she should try to understand it better. Talk about it with the teacher. If Mr. Grim teaches because he likes teenagers, ask how this year's students compare to last year's. If it's summer vacations, find out what he does with the time. Sometimes a teacher grows dull or vinegary because he has too few opportunities to talk about the positive elements of teaching—so he begins to forget what they are.

In the past month, have you tried to start a one-to-one conversation with Mr. Grim before class, after class, in the hall, at a basketball game? Do you know whether Mr. Grim has any children? any pets? Where does he shop for groceries? What library does he use? Do you know what he likes to do in his spare time? Teaching isn't all teachers do. Despite our unexamined assumptions, teachers don't spend all night in the classroom closet. Teachers enjoy being known as people. When a student asks about a teacher's out-of-school life, the student is in effect recognizing that the teacher isn't a one-dimensional paper-doll-like character, but a three-dimensional human being. That feels good.

Moreover, caring about a teacher's family life, hobbies or other interests is a way of meeting him at the level of motivations. Sometimes those questions lead to a level of values—what's important in life.

We're not saying that Mr. Grim will instantly become a brilliant and fascinating teacher once your teenager gets to know more about him as a person. But encountering him at some of the deeper levels of life may help to see and hear him with greater clarity, greater interest and, perhaps, greater understanding.

In the past month have you offered a positive comment to him? Have you ever prepared a positive surprise for your teacher? Does Mr. Grim know what you like best about his class? Like the rest of us, teachers have feelings. They thrive on lively interaction and expressed enthusiasm. If no one appreciates, no one expresses delight in the learning process, no one offers a chance to match wits or enjoy discoveries, teaching eventually goes flat.

Teaching is a public activity. If you do it well, lots of people know. If you do it poorly, lots of people know too. Teachers who rarely hear thanks or appreciation eventually lose whatever creative edge they may have once had. The zest leaves their work. Offering your interest and appreciation can restore some of the zest.

But suppose these encounters are rejected or make no difference. What then? We haven't talked about spiritual identity. Jesus, after all, suggested praying for enemies (Matthew 5:44). Praying for a dull, overbearing or wimpy teacher isn't much to ask in comparison.

We won't suggest what may happen when you pray. Prayer isn't a psychological trick, nor does it offer a drop-a-nickel-in-the-slot kind of instant and guaranteed result. But we do believe that something positive will happen. It may not be a result that's visible to anyone but you. But prayer is never without result. You can depend on it.

 CHAPTER 6

Supporting or Pushing: There's a Difference

Some parents joke—with only partly concealed bitterness—that their teenagers are "divorcing" them. These parents interpret their teenagers' efforts to establish appropriate independence as a serious and permanent breaking away. Many good, caring parents misinterpret their teenagers' need for a temporary and illusory separation from their families as a final leave-taking.

To be sure, it becomes a final leave-taking for some teenagers. But most often the separation is only temporary. How many young people do you know who, at 17, were appalled by their parents' ignorance, only to be astonished at 21 to find how much their parents have learned in four short years? As teenagers grow into adults, their parents are usually simultaneously transformed into wise and valued friends, more because of change in the child than in the parent.

Unfortunately for both parent and child, some parents throw up their hands in despair when their teenager first tries to exercise independent judgment or when the young person first shows signs of impatience with family activities and routines. Sure that they have lost all their influence over their teenager, they conclude that their parenting time is over. As a sad consequence, they abandon their responsibility to hold firmly to their own values, moral convictions, and general civilizing and socializing influence on their children. Thus, their teenager loses essential ingredients in his or her adolescent years: parental influence and guidance.

Earlier we said that parenthood, above all else, is an education in humility. No sooner do parents learn one set of things about parenting than they discover that they must let go of those things and learn new ones. At about the time your child enters secondary school, parenthood's requirements change. While you must continue to support and encourage your child to make good choices about school, you make fewer decisions about the exact route the educational journey takes.

As a result, you must begin to recognize that your child's talents and interests don't necessarily reflect your own. And you must look more closely at each contact with your teenager to distinguish times you should give firm direction and times you should leave the decision to your teenager. Allowing teenagers to make their own decisions is essential if the uniqueness God has built into these beings is to come to light and flourish.

In learning this kind of humility, parents find they must examine their own motives, values and spiritual identity. Without such a careful look at themselves, most parents will overlearn humility and give up, or will resist the lesson and court family disaster. Let's look at some examples of each.

🍎 *Humility Overdone*

Tony's mother overdoes parental humility. She has abandoned any kind of firm direction, and she helplessly caves in to her son's will. As a result, Tony has taken the upper hand in family affairs much too early. His mother calls the school saying: "Tony won't be at school today . . . No, he's not really sick. But I can't get him out of bed. I've called him several times, and he won't get up. He says he's just not going to school today."

Marie misses school a lot, and teachers notice that she's often gone on scheduled test days. No one knows whether Marie fears the tests or whether she's arranging a one-day delay so she can find out what's on the tests before taking them. Whatever the motivation, the most serious part of the story is that her father continues to write excuses to cover her absences.

Both Tony's and Marie's parents are setting effective examples for their children, but the lessons aren't good for anyone. The young people are learning that they can impose their own whims on others, that it's easy to bend the truth and get away with it, and that it's not really bad to manipulate the system for their convenience.

Some parents, it seems, sigh publicly over losing influence over their children while, inside, they feel relieved. Being a parent is hard work—having to be the constant symbol and defense of mature judgment, self-discipline, patience and support. It's no wonder some parents seem too ready to let go of the burden.

Lee's parents are that way. Lee is only 12, but his parents have essentially abandoned both him and his older sister. Though everyone still lives in the same house, the parents have turned their attention to their own jobs and their own lives. They say they've tried unsuccessfully to parent Lee, and they've given up.

When Lee's teachers declared his classroom behavior so disruptive that they could no longer deal with it while teaching the rest of the students, administrators scheduled special testing and an evaluation of the situation. Parents are always asked to attend sessions where such evaluation is discussed.

Lee's mother explained she couldn't get off work for the meeting. When the counselor called Lee's father, he also refused at first to attend. The counselor pressed further, explaining that one parent needed to be present to participate in the serious decisions being made. "I've talked with Lee about the meeting," the counselor explained, "and Lee says he'd like you to be there."

Lee's father greeted the message with a grunt of disbelief. After a brief pause, Lee's father said in a tight voice: "I've had it with those kids—both Lee and his sister. I've told them they're on their own from now on. They can live here in the house, but I'm not going to break my back trying to be a good influence on them anymore. God knows I've tried. I've . . ." His voice broke.

When he spoke again, there were tears in his voice. "I've taken him fishing, I've bought both of them all kinds of things," the father said. "But I don't get anything back from them. All I get is calls like this from school. And calls from the police because one of them is in trouble. I just haven't got any more energy to spend on those two. It's hard enough just living my own life and making ends meet . . ."

In the end, Lee's father promised to come for the meeting—to try one more time to be a supportive parent. But the meeting time came and went, and he neither appeared nor called.

At 12, Lee is essentially orphaned. Having failed to establish an identity or attract attention in positive ways, he has resorted to negative ways, and his parents have given up. Most likely, his parents truly wanted to be good parents at one time. But they didn't know how to go about it. And so—having experienced failure after failure in parenting—they've stopped trying. They've too easily grasped the label "Failed Parent" and have turned their backs.

Lee, too, has failed to find the firm but caring attention every child needs. And now, even before reaching the teenage years, he has suffered a devastating loss: His parents have abandoned him.

One wonders how different the story would be if the parents had accepted the idea that they were entrusted with two children of God, and had treated them with the attention, firmness, respect and support they therefore should have had.

Humility Resisted

The parents who most often find their way to the school principal's or counselor's office are parents who resist the lesson of humility. They're intent on keeping their teenager on a short leash. Believing they know what's best for their child, they want to be as fully involved in their youngster's decisions as possible—just as they were in elementary school. They want to advise on (read "choose") their child's electives. They ask to be informed if their child fails to hand in an assigned piece of homework (an unreasonable request, in most cases, since some school staff person would have to monitor five or six courses each day).

And they push.

Pushing is different from supporting. Support recognizes that, in growing toward adulthood, a teenager must do some things uninstructed, make some decisions unsupervised, make some trial runs at independence. Support waits to cheer or comfort, depending on the outcome. To be sure, encouragement is a part of support. But pushing moves beyond encouragement (a background role) into the foreground of deciding, directing, insisting.

Are You Pushing Too Hard?

One thing that makes being a parent difficult is that teenagers don't come with pressure gauges. It would be convenient if they were equipped with some accurate, visible device—something on the order of a barometer—so parents could tell when their encouragement about school performance has gone beyond "helpful" to the "danger zone."

However, thus far we haven't developed a reliable gadget to warn us to ease off the pressure on our children. And unfortunately, some kinds of encouragement, when overdone, are likely to produce the opposite of what we were hoping for.

In Search Institute's survey of young adolescents and their parents, we discovered that most teenagers recognize that a reasonable level of parental "pushing" is helpful. Roughly two-thirds of the young people agree that both their father and mother push them to do their best in whatever they do.[1] The atmosphere in most of these homes appears to be healthy. Many of these students say their parents treat them with affection, try to be democratic about rule-setting, and talk reasonably with their children about misbehavior.

At the same time, a smaller percentage of students (19 percent of boys and 16 percent of girls) say their parents "expect too much of me," and they also speak of an authoritarian parenting style that lays down the law and sees that teenagers toe the line.[2] If these young people wore pressure gauges, the needles would point to "danger."

Jeff Jordan was built like his father, well-muscled and tall. By ninth grade, he was 6 feet 1 inch and growing. An avid basketball fan, Jeff's father was delighted that his son had the potential to be an outstanding basketball player. He'd be a star in high school, make a brilliant record in college, and perhaps even go on to the pros. By the time Jeff was in fifth grade, his father had installed a hoop on the garage and was spending many hours coaching Jeff, shooting baskets and talking about ball-handling techniques.

At first, Jeff enjoyed his father's attention, and he participated quite willingly in the practice sessions. But as he grew taller and his father's demands grew sharper and more exacting, Jeff's interest began to wane. As soon as the boy moved into high school, Jeff's father contacted the high school basketball coach, who was also impressed with Jeff's potential. By the fall of his 10th-grade year, both the coach and Jeff's father were working hard to persuade a now-reluctant Jeff to try out for varsity basketball.

But Jeff didn't turn out for practices. He was evasive and non-committal as they urged him. "C'mon, Jeff. You owe it to your school. You'd be one of the great ones." "You'd make us all proud of you. Jeff Jordan would

"What do you mean, you're not cut out to be
a pro basketball player?"

become a household name. You've got the real stuff. We've just got to hone your skills a little more . . ."

Jeff began hanging around the school theater at the end of the day, almost as if seeking someplace—anyplace—to hide from the pressure. He discovered he also had some aptitude for drama, and an alert teacher allowed him to develop it. During his remaining high school years he worked backstage on many productions and appeared on stage several times.

But after ninth grade, Jeff never appeared on a high school basketball court except for required physical education courses. However, in his senior year when he played Riff in *West Side Story*, all 6 feet 5 inches of him danced with the strength, timing and grace of a born athlete.

Jeff didn't come with a built-in gauge that told his father he was pushing too hard. But signals were being sent, though Mr. Jordan had been too absorbed in pursuing his own goal to notice them.

It's important to be alert to the signals when parental pressure becomes too intense. And it's important for parents to be clear about the motives and interests that may cause them to be overly concerned about their teenager's academic performance, and push too hard. The following questions point to some clues:

1. Are there changes in your teenager's ☐ Yes ☐ No behavior or health (such as disturbed sleep, upset stomach, loss of appetite, or headaches) as report-card time approaches?

2. Do you expect your teenager to do ☐ Yes ☐ No everything at the highest possible level for her or him?

3. When your teenager's performance ☐ Yes ☐ No shows improvement, do you usually say something such as: "See? Didn't I tell you you could do better? Now if you'd only try harder, you could . . .'"?

4. Do you feel as if, over an extended ☐ Yes ☐ No time period, you've been putting more energy than your teenager into accomplishing what your teenager needs to do?

5. When you're talking with your teenager about the area where you may be pushing too hard, does he or she sometimes send resistance signals (heavy sighs, turning away, expressing anger, walking away)? ☐ Yes ☐ No

6. Have you promised your teenager a prize or monetary reward for grades you think are appropriate? ☐ Yes ☐ No

7. Do you concentrate on one child's abilities more than those of your other children? ☐ Yes ☐ No

8. When one of your other children taunts your teenager about poor performance in a subject or sport, do you find yourself silently cheering? ☐ Yes ☐ No

9. Would it embarrass you to have your friends know your teenager's level of academic performance? ☐ Yes ☐ No

Distress at grading time. *Are there changes in your teenager's behavior or health as report-card time approaches?*

One of the first signs of trouble to watch for is serious distress over schoolwork that becomes more intense at grade time. Look beneath the behavior to the worries that compel it.

It's usual and normal for teenagers to be anxious at test time. Even the best-prepared students feel some anxiety before tests. They know a question could be asked that they didn't anticipate, and they worry about a memory failure at a crucial time. However, if the anxiety is extreme, that's a danger signal.

Some students generate their own pressure over tests. If your teenager is among them, don't ignore the physical signs. Ask questions about wants and worries. "Is this test more important than others you've taken?" "What do you think is the worst that could happen because of this test?" "How serious an effect would 'the worst' have on you?"

While test anxiety may be normal, if the anxiety is more noticeable around grade time than test time, you as a parent may be pushing too hard. The signs may be saying that your teenager is afraid of your disapproval if the grades aren't up to your standards—whether the standards are explicitly stated or only implied.

If you suspect such a fear, ask about motivation. "Are you anxious about your grades?" "Are you afraid your grades will disappoint me, or are you just worried about being disappointed yourself?" When asked in a tone that conveys support, not judgment, questions such as these can help your teenager state the fears aloud and then deal with them, rather than letting them buzz around inside his or her head like bothersome insects.

After these questions about motivation may come a "values" question: "Whom is it more important to please with what you do in school: yourself or me?" Telling your feelings to your teenager at the level of goals and values isn't easy. But the consequences of such talk will likely bring rewards in the forms of further understanding and greater family closeness.

Unrealistic expectations. *Do you expect your teenager to do everything at the highest possible level for her or him?*

If your teenager is good at some things but not others, that's normal. We aren't all high-achievers at everything. Appreciate what your teenager *is* good at. Foster it. Feel good about it. Try not to mourn the gifts your teenager wasn't given.

We recognize unrealistic expectations in adult life, but we're often less apt to see the unrealistic expectations we have for teenagers. Taken across the board, we can't reasonably live adult life at top form in every category. When people plan a backpacking trip, the lawn care tends to slip. When the good Samaritan stopped to take care of the man who fell among thieves (Luke 10:30-36), whoever was expecting him at his destination had to wait a while. When people write books, they tend to dine on frozen dinners a lot. When Dad directs evening rehearsals for the church play, he doesn't spend half an hour every night reading aloud to the children.

We make choices and trade-offs throughout life. Teenagers have a right to the same freedom to express priorities. Maybe this term the main focus should be English, since that seems to be the problem. So if the general science grade stays where it was last time, that may be all anyone—parent or teenager—can reasonably expect. Setting your sights too high almost certainly guarantees failure.

Raising the bar. *When your teenager's performance shows improvement, do you usually say something such as: "See? Didn't I tell you you could do better? Now if you'd only try harder, you could . . ."?*

We mentioned earlier some parents' disheartening tendency to raise the bar a notch above whatever level the teenager has managed to achieve. It's a cruel but common pressure: to make students feel that whatever they do isn't enough.

Some parents have an insatiable greed for more and bigger academic trophies. When the young person has finally finished school—having cleared all the academic hurdles, garnered all the trophies—the pressure continues. There is still pressure (though it may be more subtle) for higher and higher salaries or greater and greater honors. Such demands often result in a permanent rift between apparently loving parents and their high-achieving children. And sometimes the demands have, in effect, shaped their children into permanently dissatisfied trophy-chasers.

Such was the case with one hard-nosed, financially successful and profoundly unhappy executive we know. We heard him discovering, at age 50, with a rush of cleansing tears: "My father died 15 years ago. But I still push and push and drive myself and everybody around me so that someday I'll be good enough, finally, to please my dad."

Psychologist Bruno Bettelheim suggests that much

parent-child alienation occurs because of constantly rising expectations. Children come to believe that their parents care more about the symbols of success their children can give them than they do about their child.[3]

When our teenagers perceive such tendencies in us, we deprive them of the thing that they deeply hunger for and that only parents can supply: the sense that no matter what happens, their parents love, appreciate and support them.

What happened to your teenager's own motivation? *Do you feel as if, over an extended time period, you've been putting more energy than your teenager into accomplishing what your teenager needs to do? When you're talking with your teenager about the area where you may be pushing too hard, does he or she sometimes send resistance signals (heavy sighs, turning away, expressing anger, walking away)? Have you promised your teenager a prize or monetary reward for grades you think are appropriate?*

Teenagers who do well academically get lots of goodies. According to Bettelheim: "The child who does well academically earns many rewards; his parents are pleased with him, his teachers praise him, he receives good grades. Thus if a child who has the requisite abilities to succeed in school nevertheless fails, there must be very powerful reasons at work which cause his failure, reasons which, to the child, are clearly more compelling than the rewards for academic success."[4]

If you answered yes to the three questions just listed, something is wrong. It's normal for teenagers to want to do well academically—just as it's normal for adult workers to want to do their jobs well. The signals in the three questions clearly indicate that you are more interested in your teenager's academic success than he or she is, and that your teenager is resisting your taking over part of his or her own life.

If a parent must spend more time and energy arranging for a teenager to study than the teenager actually spends studying; if the teenager sends signals of resistance; and if a parent must offer rewards to coax a teenager to do what he or she ought naturally to want to do, something has gotten in the way.

For many parents, paying for grades seems like a logical reward when their teenagers do well. In an informal survey of 400 teenagers at the 1988 National Christian Youth Congress, one out of five young people said their parents give them money for good grades. One senior said she receives $10 for every A. Another said that if she gets a 4.0 grade point average at the end of the year, she gets $1,000.

It seems to us that paying for grades does more harm than good. Several problems come to mind:

1. Interest in learning and academic success should be intrinsic, not a means to another end. When parents pay teenagers for high grades, the grade—the symbol—becomes the focus, usurping the appropriate focus on learning.

2. Giving a monetary reward reinforces the idea that the grades belong to the parents. It makes parents the con-sumers of grades and the student the supplier, receiving fees for grades delivered (or services rendered).

3. When educators ask for volunteers to help on a school project and a teenager asks, "What do I get for it?" they know that he or she has been taught to expect exter-nal payoff. If the attitude persists, that teenager will never be able to enjoy the simple pleasure of helping someone else or the camaraderie of joining a group to achieve a cooperative goal. Unless something changes, that teenager will become an adult who probably won't volunteer for any kind of community responsibility, who won't give gen-erously to the church or other good causes simply because he or she believes in them, and who won't become a dependable and favorite neighbor. Instead, that person will continually be asking, "What's in it for me?"

4. It's only a short step from being paid for good grades (or punished for poor ones) to encouraging students to use any means necessary to get the desired grades. As a result, paying for grades encourages cheating.

Cheating is worrisomely widespread nowadays. And it occurs primarily because children have been taught to believe that the grade—the symbol—is more valuable than the learning. The frequency of cheating indicates that parents believe grades are the major prize, that they have mistaken the symbol for substance, and that they have passed that mistaken belief on to their children.

The topic of cheating is a good one for opening a family discussion of how values become evident in behavior. Values sometimes conflict. Everyone enjoys winning, and winning says nice things about the winner. But if your teenager declares that cheating is necessary for a particular win, then it's time to talk about the relative values of honesty and achievement.

Are you playing favorites? *Do you concentrate on one child's abilities more than those of your other children?*

Having more than one child in the family has its rewards, but it also creates potential problems. One of the chief difficulties is the potential for inequitable treatment. And one temptation that leads to such treatment is to have one child whose gifts or problems mark that child as different from the others.

If you concentrate more of either praise or concern on one child, the other children will know it and resent it. Of course, circumstances may dictate that you can't always spend equal amounts of time and attention with each child's progress in school. However, if one child's situation requires more from you than you give to the other children, be aware of the disparity. Acknowledge your awareness to the other children, and ask them to talk with you about their feelings. Your awareness of the inequality should also alert you to the need for special strokes for those who probably feel left out and ignored.

A child's desire to be valued and loved by his or her parents is so strong that, even when he or she understands intellectually the need to focus more strongly on a brother or sister, it *feels* bad. Having that feeling acknowledged—

and not being required to cover or deny those feelings—
will go a long way toward healing the hurts of the
neglected ones.

If one of your children seems to have a learning problem, consult your school counselors and administrators. Request evaluations and a diagnosis. Ask the school to create
a special education program to deal with the problem
(Chapter 9). The process will necessarily require spending
unequal amounts of time on your children's educations—
perhaps only temporarily, perhaps permanently.

*When one of your other children taunts your teenager
about poor performance in a subject or sport, do you
find yourself silently cheering?*

This question also deals with sibling rivalry, but only
as the secondary issue. The primary issue is your own reaction. If you are inwardly pleased that you hear the taunts,
examine your motives. Do you assume sibling pressure will
result in more or better work from your targeted teenager?
Or are you disappointed and frustrated about the teenager's
performance and therefore feeling grateful to have an ally?

If your own efforts to improve performance haven't
achieved the goal, the teasing will likely result in less
achievement, not more. Teenagers who have failed to meet
a standard—either their own or one set by others—are
already punishing themselves sufficiently. Drawing further
attention to the failure makes things worse, not better.

*Would it embarrass you to have your friends know
your teenager's level of academic performance?*

If you answered yes to this question, it indicates two
things. First, it says you are disappointed because your
teenager hasn't performed up to your own standards. Second, it says your own ego is wrapped up in your teenager's
achievements. That brings us back to the matter of
ownership.

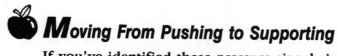

Moving From Pushing to Supporting

If you've identified these pressure signals in your own

teenager, your Amy is likely receiving the message that her grades don't belong to her. In order to remedy the situation, you must stop resisting the lesson of humility.

Before you can make constructive changes in your relationship with Amy, you must first settle your own identity. You are not God. You are not in charge of the universe. You may have helped create this child's life, but you are not solely responsible. So you don't have to guarantee results. Instead, you must give up the idea of ownership, while continuing to appreciate and support.

How do you begin? Simply changing your tactics without explanation may make Amy suspicious. It's more honest to sit down with her and explain that you want to change the way you try to help her with her education. Explain why.

Affirm that you now believe her schooling is her business, not yours. And, while you will be supportive and help when she asks for help, you're going to treat her more like an adult. You know you can't control her forever, and what she does with her school assignments is up to her. Of course, you still want her to do well, and you believe she has the ability. But her day-to-day stewardship of her God-given talents is up to her. You're not going to push anymore.

Then comes the hard part: You have to do it. You have to keep hands off. Your goal should be not to even know what the assignments are. If your past habits are too strong, you can begin by changing the nature of your questions about school. Instead of asking, "What are your English assignments for this week?" (a question an owner would ask), try, "What are you doing in English this week?" If it's reading, ask if she likes the reading, and why. If it's grammar, ask if it's any easier for her now than it was earlier. Those are the questions of an interested parent.

If you get an answer, that's your quota of information for the week. If you don't get an answer, let it go. If you're ready to give up your pattern of close supervision in hopes of better long-term results (including qualities not marked on a report card), you can't expect your teenager to turn over a new leaf right away. Your teenager is the way he or she is in part because of your family's history, and that history can't be wiped out overnight. What you are doing now, in effect, is beginning to write a new history that can provide a better background for your relationship with your teenager.

Learning to exercise humility takes time. It's a difficult discipline. After a period of testing your genuineness, Amy may feel more like telling you things without prompting. It doesn't always happen, but it does reasonably often.

Let's add a caution: Don't back off so far that you give the impression that you've given up on your teenager or have abandoned him or her. We've observed some parents who gave up their pattern of too-close supervision only to swing so vigorously to the opposite extreme that their children resented it. Both verbally and non-verbally, these parents turned very cool. Their words and actions said: "Okay. From now on it's up to you. I'm going to stay out of your affairs. It's up to you whether you fail or pass. It's none of my business anymore."

The message is almost right, but it lacks two critical ingredients. It lacks the promise of caring support and encouragement, and it fails to convey that the parents sincerely want to learn the parental lesson of humility.

🍎 *Why Parents Don't Always Know Best*

There's another good reason for Christian parents to let their teenagers make their own decisions about their education. To assume the role of decision-maker for our children assumes a level of omniscience that none of us has. As we keep discovering from day to day, we human creatures retain throughout life our incompleteness, our frailty, our shortsightedness.

Not everything we've done as parents has produced stellar results. Not all of our personal qualities are without fault. In our case, we didn't need to duplicate Lyle and

Dorothy in our children. Lyle takes too long to tell a story, and Dorothy is woefully impatient. The world doesn't cry out for two more of us. Why shouldn't we hope for something better—something entirely new—in our children, without insisting that we decide or control what form that newness takes?

Time after time, we've seen parents discovering that imposed decisions that seemed right at the time proved, in the end, to be wrong. And time after time, we've seen teenagers who refused to follow their parents' carefully mapped routes for them do very well indeed.

Scott's parents are both college graduates, both educators. Quite naturally, they expected Scott to enter college after high school. Obediently, but reluctantly, he enrolled. He toiled his way through the freshman year, but the work was obviously tedious and dull to him.

At year's end, after consulting with his parents, he left college and enrolled in technical school. There he found studying food preparation much more to his liking.

At the end of his study, Scott took a position with a hotel chain, and shortly thereafter, was sent by the company to Switzerland for a special course in Swiss pastries. Scott still receives not only a substantial salary, but considerable satisfaction in his work—as well as fairly regular offers to take other head-chef positions in other parts of the country.

If we insist on seeing our children throughout their school careers make choices based on our adult advice, we close off the possibility of something much different— sometimes much better—than we would have dreamed of or chosen. Insisting on our own way reduces our openness to God's creativity. By our insistence, we essentially foreclose on the God ". . . who is able to do immeasurably more than all we ask or imagine, according to his power that is at work within us" (Ephesians 3:20).

God isn't finished with creation. God continues to create all around us. God isn't finished with you, nor is he finished with your teenager. Why should we not, then, more fully entrust the supremely important direction of the life of this teenager—who we have so hopefully nurtured—to God's loving and creative power?

CHAPTER 7

Basic Study Skills and Tools

Most teenagers want to learn. That may be difficult to believe when your 13-year-old fails to complete eight math assignments in one term, never brings home a book, and declares that school is "booooring." But believe it. Your child may find achievement easier in basketball than in biology, but every young person wants to achieve at something—and most would prefer, if they could, to do well in everything.

Unhappily, some teenagers don't know how to achieve in school. While many teenagers have picked up the necessary skills along the way through the help of a parent, a good teacher, a helpful older brother or sister or a friend, many haven't. And without the necessary skills these young people struggle along, frustrated by their inability to achieve. That frustration leads to apathy and feelings of failure.

If your teenager hasn't picked up the skills—no matter how far advanced in school he or she is—it's time for some help. Of course, helping doesn't mean taking over. As you discover your teenager's hopes regarding education, offer to help your teenager achieve those goals by working together on learning skills. Your posture should be that of a coach who offers suggestions to players to see if the ideas will increase a batting average. As is true with a coach in sports, if the suggestions are genuinely tried for a reasonable period of time but don't seem to work, there's no need to continue them.

By suggesting ways to use test time wisely, recommending ways to relax, and pointing out what to do first, you're taking the appropriate role of coach. You're making suggestions from the sidelines, but both you and your teenager recognize that the success or failure of this particular step of learning rests on the teenager's shoulders. And that is exactly as it should be.

When you offer to help, your teenager may greet the offer with suspicion. A teenager who hasn't yet acquired good study skills is probably conscious that something is lacking. He or she may react defensively, feeling that any offer of help implies a deficiency. Meet the defensive response gently: "I didn't mean to sound as if I'm criticizing you. I've just been reading some things about studying that I wish I'd known when I was in school, and I thought you might like to know about them." Patience and persistence are essential. If you get a cold shoulder at first, wait a little while and raise the subject again.

In this chapter we offer you and your teenager some simple, basic learning suggestions that have helped many students and parents. Try them and keep the useful ones. But if they don't work after a reasonable trial period, there's no need to continue them. If you discover study problems deeper than you had imagined, seek help from a qualified school counselor.

🍎 The Importance of Reading

A teenager's interest in reading is a strong indicator of that teenager's success in school. Show us a teenager who devours library books by the armful, who reads by flashlight under bedcovers when lights are supposed to be out, who carries a book along when going to visit a friend "just in case I have to wait," and we'll show you someone who has excellent potential for good grades in most academic subjects.

When parents of young children learn about the connection between reading and grades, they respond by surrounding their children with reading material. Parents who themselves read a lot set an excellent example for their children, and parents who read to their preschooler not only enjoy the experience, but set an excellent foundation for the time the child begins to read in school.

But what about a junior high student who doesn't like to read—for whom all encounters with the printed page are a chore? How can parents help such a teenager enjoy reading?

Here's a method that has improved some teenagers' reading skills—and sometimes their grades. If you have a reluctant reader in your family, try it.

1. Get thee to the public library. Ask the librarian to show you the magazines teenagers commonly read. Take home one or two issues of a selection of magazines. Don't take home any that you wouldn't want seen lying around your house, but don't confine the selection to your own personal interests either. Even if you're not interested in car racing or skiing or knitting, take those magazines home if your teenager shows interest in those subjects.

2. Show the magazines to your teenager (or just let the magazines lie around conspicuously for a while). Ask (or observe) which ones he or she seems to enjoy most or spends the most time with.

3. Subscribe to one or two of the favored magazines— in your teenager's name. In time, the magazines of interest begin to arrive. Almost all teenagers are drawn into that kind of reading. And the reading process has begun.

4. If the initial investment in a subscription seems worthwhile, try another one. Sometimes (not always, but sometimes) the enthusiasm and facility of reading derived from pleasure-reading spreads to more academic reading. Most good readers began by reading for fun. Perhaps it will happen for your teenager.

Too many parents, hoping to encourage their children to read, buy expensive sets of the classics. After a few days, these collections gather dust on the shelves. The intentions

"They're for my teenager . . ."

are good, but the result is disappointing. Try the inexpensive subscription instead. Granted, Car and Driver magazine isn't great literature. But it has a better chance than the classics of getting your non-reading teenager started.

Reading for school. In addition to the value of general reading for education, it's important for young people to know how most efficiently to use their reading time in school subjects. One good method, in use for several decades in some schools, is called the SQ3R method. The acronym represents five activities: survey, question, read, recite, review. This method for absorbing written material makes better use of reading time than the casual read-through most students give their reading assignments.

Survey. When the teacher assigns a chapter to read, the natural tendency is to open the book and start reading at the beginning. However, that's not the most productive way to go about it. Think of a chapter as a jigsaw puzzle. A puzzle is easier to solve when we have a general idea of what the entire picture looks like. Knowing the subject, it's easier to fit the pieces together. So it is with reading.

The first task: Read the title and guess from it what the topic is. Then look through the chapter, reading only the section heads. If there are any, look at the pictures, charts or illustrations.

Question. Ask yourself questions about what the set of headings means. Read the conclusion or summary (if one is given), and ask yourself questions about that too. How can you start out there and wind up here? What caused such a great change? What's the point of all that?

Read. Begin reading only when you have a general picture of the chapter's overall content and some questions in mind. As you read, you're filling out a skeleton of what you already know about the chapter's content. And you're looking for answers to your questions.

Recite. When you've finished reading (before you put the book down and go on to something else), write a summary of what the chapter told you. (This process is a do-it-yourself "reciting.") How much you write depends on

(a) how interested you are in it, and (b) this chapter's importance to the whole course. Sometimes a sentence or two is enough. Sometimes you need a sentence or two about each section within the chapter. Also, most reading assignments are discussed in class the next day. Participate in this recitation.

Review. After a day or two, see how much of the information you can remember without looking at your summary. Then check your memory by looking at your notes. If you couldn't remember your summary very well, take time to review the whole chapter again and revise your summary.

Tools and Organization

Another requirement for school achievement is having a set of proper, well-organized tools. If your teenager doesn't know how to organize learning materials—whether he or she is in seventh grade or about to graduate from high school—it's time to learn.

As anybody knows who has ever tried to turn an ordinary screw with a Phillips screwdriver, the right equipment makes a big difference. The same is true with school-work—it's much easier with the right equipment. Let's look at some essential equipment for a student's toolbox:

Notebooks. One essential piece of equipment is something to manage the papers that school generates. Although some students use other methods (a two-pocket folder or spiral notebook for each subject, large wads of paper stuffed into jeans pockets or crammed helter-skelter into the backpack) a three-ring notebook works best.

Choose a notebook with an inside diameter ring size of at least 1¼-inches to hold enough papers without mutilating them in the process. Insert properly labeled dividers ("Math," "English," "Social Studies" and so on) to bring order to the welter of papers that soon collects.

Pencil pouch. Keep pencils (note: pencils—plural), pens, a 6-inch ruler, compass and other tools secure in a durable plastic, zippered pencil pouch inside the notebook. Pencils in hip pockets are inviting candidates for others to snatch away; loose pencils in textbooks or notebooks get dropped.

Extra paper. Store an adequate supply of three-hole notebook paper at the front or back of the notebook. Fifty sheets are plenty; there's no need to overcrowd. Keep the rest at home for refills when the notebook paper runs low.

Assignment sheets. At the front of the notebook, keep three or four assignment sheets that look something like Diagram 3. If you wish, you may photocopy this diagram for your own use. Have your teenager put the dates of the three coming weeks at the tops, and then record *every assignment* on the sheets.

The key word on the assignment sheet is "due." When the math teacher announces on Wednesday, "Your assignment for tomorrow is . . .," the student writes that information in the space on the "math" line for Thursday. And when the geography teacher announces on the same day that "we will finish this unit next Monday and the unit test will be Tuesday," the student flips to the next week's sheet and writes in the "Due Tuesday" column "Test, Unit 6."

It's important to record every assignment, even if the student expects to complete it during the current class period. The student should also record on the sheet predictable activities, even if unannounced by the teacher—the every-Friday spelling test, the every-Tuesday lab, the Monday current-events quiz. When the young person completes an assignment or takes a test, he or she then crosses out the assignment or test on the schedule.

If there isn't a math assignment for Tuesday, the student should note in that space what happened in Tuesday's math class. Teenagers can be wonderfully creative about why blanks appear on the sheet—"We didn't do anything that day," or, "We were working on the project." Ask your teenager to write in activities such as "worked on wood project" or "film on Bolivia" or "corrected test." The record of assignments and day-to-day happenings is just

Diagram 3

Daily Assignment Sheet

Week of _____

Period	Due Monday	Due Tuesday	Due Wednesday	Due Thursday	Due Friday

what the student needs for periodic review.

This whole process yields several benefits:

1. Writing down an assignment helps the student remember it.

2. Students find considerable satisfaction in crossing off a completed assignment. (Some adults even add already-completed tasks to their "to do" list so they can have the small reward of crossing them off!)

3. The sheet also provides a ready-made pack-for-home list when the student leaves school for the day.

4. Finally, the record is an excellent memory jogger when it's time to prepare for a test.

Make sure your teenager never discards a sheet until all assignments are completed. Even when everything on the sheet is complete, keep it in a folder at home until the end of the marking period. Unfortunately, some students feel justified in discarding last week's sheet because that was last week—whether or not the assignments were properly completed. Keeping the old assignment sheets saves the teacher the trouble of listing missing assignments at mid-term reckoning time and the trouble of a parent calling to get a list of uncompleted work.

This system will sound elementary to students who've been keeping such a record for years. But if your teenager doesn't have a similar system, get one started. It's simple and works beautifully—as long as it's used. And it's worth taking the time and adding a few ounces to your image as the "Heavy Parent" to be sure that your teenager knows the system and has the equipment to put it into action. At junior high age, at least, you may want to follow up your initial conversation about this system with periodic checks to determine whether the system is being used properly.

 **H**omework

Most schools assume that students will spend some time at home completing schoolwork. Teenagers who do homework most effectively are those who (a) have some say in deciding where and when the work gets done, and (b) have their family's cooperation.

How much time? How much time does the average student need at home for schoolwork? Figures collected nationally by Search Institute indicate that, at ninth grade, students are divided into thirds. The first third spend two hours or less a week, the next third spend from three to five hours, and the final third, six hours or more a week.[1] Another national study of public school 12th-graders has found that students spend the following amounts of time doing homework:

- One to three hours per week: 30 percent
- Three to five hours per week: 21 percent
- Five to 10 hours per week: 18 percent
- Eleven or more hours per week: 6 percent[2]

These are national averages, and your teenager's situation may call for reasonable variations. School counselors, administrators or teachers can help you with that judgment. The amount of time will vary from day to day, of course, but it's rather simple to determine a minimum.

By the end of the first three weeks of school, you should be able to get a fairly accurate estimate of the homework load for those particular classes. If, during that period, you see almost no work brought home, the warning flag goes up. Begin asking questions without delay.

When your teenager has a feel for the term's homework load, talk together about a minimum time to set aside each night for schoolwork. Come to a joint decision on an appropriate time, and decide together to honor your agreement. If changes seem necessary in a few weeks, agree to renegotiate.

Schedule a Quiet Time. Suppose you and your teenager agree on a minimum of 40 minutes per day. Next, decide on a schedule, preferably in a family meeting. A joint decision is better because study time needs to be a scheduled Quiet Time for the entire family. A teenager who hasn't followed a disciplined study schedule will have an easier time beginning one when all family activity quiets down during study time. Parents can read the paper, relax with a good novel or pay bills; younger siblings can color, read or work on projects.

It's hard to study when someone else insists on watching television during Quiet Time. Therefore, include the whole family in choosing the time, considering TV programming, piano practicing and other scheduled commitments. Then make a chart showing when the 40-minute period falls each weekday, and post it on the refrigerator door or another equally obvious place.

If all family members have had a voice in the decision and each member's needs have been heard, your negotiated schedule should be successful. And if, after a trial period, adjustments seem advisable, make them in another family meeting.

Agree as a family that study time will always occur on schedule. Observe Quiet Time even if your teenager contends: "I have absolutely no homework. I did it all in study time at school." If your teenager wants to avoid staring at the walls during the time, the remedy is to have work to do—reread the social studies chapter, review science notes, read ahead on the next book report, or read schoolwork-related material with or without extra credit.

If you find after a few weeks of Quiet Time that schoolwork gets done promptly and well, discuss with your teenager whether it's time to reduce the length of time or abandon it altogether, allowing the teenager to arrange study time without the family's help. If family cooperation was what your teenager needed, chances are about even that he or she will ask to continue Quiet Time. If you choose to abandon the schedule, make it clear that Quiet Time will be reinstated if the teenager doesn't manage her or his time well enough to get the necessary work done.

Location. Where is the best place for home study? Trying to arrange the best possible study environment, many parents buy attractive and costly study centers for their teenager's room. Unfortunately, these centers often do no more than collect stereo equipment or miscellaneous heaps of clothing.

The well-equipped teenager often studies in the kitchen or at the dining room table. Curiously enough, these familiar and busy spots are hands-down favorites with most students. Students who like their families want to be near them. It's no fun being isolated in your room if you like knowing what else is going on in the house. (After all, didn't the severe order, "Go to your room!" amount to punishment in elementary days?)

Studying in a public space is also better from a parent's point of view. It allows you to sense frustration, and offer help and answer questions when the student is nearby. It's also easier to get a sense of what's going on—real work as opposed to sitting and staring—when you don't have to invade the privacy of your teenager's bedroom to find out.

Class Participation

The classroom is the crucible for many important elements of the learning process. If the student doesn't use classroom time well, trouble occurs later on—missed assignments, explanations not written down, test material that comes as a surprise.

Sooner or later, teenagers must learn to attend to instruction—film, lecture, demonstration, explanation or class discussion. They must learn about listening critically, and they must make judgments about note-taking, constantly asking whether what they hear is important enough to write down. Let's look at keys to using classroom time well.

Concentration. Concentration is essential to excellence everywhere. And the young person who wants to succeed anywhere, at anything, must learn how to concentrate. The first rule to good classroom work is to put aside all extraneous interests and activities so you can concentrate on the teacher's directions and assigned activities.

There are plenty of diversions. The room is full of Ginas looking for mirrors and would-be comedians seeking the spotlight. Serious students must learn to screen out those distractions. During class, they avoid conversations with friends, personal note-writing, personal artwork and leisure reading—three attractive distractions.

Different subjects require different types of concentration. In art, music, physical education, home economics, mass media, industrial technology and science laboratories, for example, you need a concentrated, steady effort at the work station toward completing the project, improving the skill or perfecting the artistic presentation. The teacher can easily see and hear what's going on. The teacher knows whether a student is working on a back flip, sanding a piece of wood or delivering the next line in the play. It's not difficult to monitor students' concentration in these courses.

However, work in the academic classroom is largely invisible to the teacher because much of it occurs inside the students' heads. Thus only the student is responsible for concentrating. If a student fails to take that responsibility, the reckoning day will come.

Participatory listening. During most lectures or demonstrations, words come at us at only about 150 to 175 words per minute—several times slower than the rate the mind can absorb information. Anticipating the next point or drawing tentative conclusions from presentations sharpens comprehension skills. With practice, we can train our minds to dart ahead, anticipate, relate and consider parallel meanings—all of which make us more productive listeners.

Note-taking. Knowing how to take good notes is a useful skill throughout life—whether the "notes" are written or only recorded in the memory. Note-taking is a fairly complex process involving:

- hearing what is being said,
- getting an overall grasp of its meaning,
- and selecting what to record in memory or on paper.

Almost all students need to be shown why note-taking

is an important skill and how to do it. It's a teachable skill, and understanding its importance motivates students to learn how to do it. They discover how much easier it is to keep track in class when they know how to take notes well.

If your teenager isn't being taught how to take notes in school, you can step in and help. But maybe nobody taught you either. If so, see what you and your teenager can figure out together. In at least an informal sense, you've been hearing, grasping meaning and selecting what to retain in memory for a long time. You probably know more than you think you do.

Here's an exercise you can try together:

1. Large helpings of information are being dished out to us all the time. Agree with your teenager on some public presentation—like a newscast—for a chance to practice note-taking together. Other good sources of information include sermons, campaign speeches and committee meetings.

2. Listen together, without consulting each other. Record what you think are the major points covered in the newscast or presentation.

3. Afterward, compare notes. How much did each of you write down? Did you generally agree on what were the most important elements of what you heard?

4. Find out what your differences are. Don't assume what you chose to record is right and anything else is wrong. Determining rights and wrongs will doom the process. If your teenager chose to note something you missed, comment positively. "Hey! I missed that. Good for you!"

5. Discuss why each of you decided what was worth recording. Again, don't assume that what you're doing is automatically right. If your teenager *hears* your criteria for choosing and they make sense, you don't have to pound in the learning with a hammer. And if your criteria don't make sense, your teenager probably wouldn't remember them anyway.

For example, in watching a newscast, your teenager might not take notes on a crop failure in the Farm Belt. When you ask why, he or she might say, "Because we live in Vermont." But you could explain that a crop failure in Iowa *is* important to you because it could result in increased prices for food in your supermarket.

6. Try the exercise again a few days later. See if your agreement improves, or if you can teach each other anything further this time.

7. Then try it once again. Without reading them, put your notes away for a while (a day is good; a week is better). Then compare. How much of what you wrote can each of you still remember? Is there any unnecessary motion in your note-taking? For example, are you writing down unnecessary words (articles, transitions and so forth) that slow you down? Have you written enough so that you can still figure out what the note means, but not so much that you missed the next item? Letting your notes get cold is an excellent test of whether your teenager will be able to make sense of class notes a month later at review time.

🍎 *Taking Tests*

Test time emphasizes to parents that school experience and performance really do belong to the teenager, not the parent. No matter how eager parents are to help their students, they have to accept the reality that the student is the one who takes the test and has to live with the results. Helping your teenager get ready for tests is one of the best ways you can support your teenager's learning.

Most people think of tests as necessary evils. Tests are efficient vehicles for finding out how much of the course material students have absorbed and how much has vanished. Like grades, they're what we have to use until something better comes along.

Most students are nervous about taking tests. Well-prepared students may feel quite calm, but—in order not to seem "holier than thou" to other students—may echo the prevailing cry that they're terrified of the upcoming exam. (There's an amusing contradiction there: Although students often report in anonymous surveys feeling pressure from their friends to keep their grades up, they still feel that they must pretend to be completely unprepared.)

Aside from putting up appearances, the degree of *real* anxiety is usually in direct proportion to the lack of preparation. If a test consisted only of items such as the student's home telephone number, shoe size and mother's first name, few students would be anxious beforehand. But when students fear the test will cover material they can't remember or have never fully understood, they're understandably anxious.

Several practical suggestions can make life much less panic-ridden for those who dread tests. Try these:

Prepare for the test. The key to an anxiety-free test day is preparation. No matter how well your teenager studies when learning new material, he or she will have to study extra for tests. None of us retains more than a fraction of what we read or hear. In fact, we lose about 80 percent of the details of what we hear within 24 hours of learning them.[3] Thus review is essential. The only question is how frequently reviewing should occur. The rate of forgetting is slowed dramatically if periodic reviews take place a day or two after the original learning, and then again a week later.[4]

Ideally, students begin getting ready for the next test the day after the preceding one is over. Teenagers should take good notes, complete assignments as soon as they are given (because that way they fit in better with class activities and what the students are reading), and review notes at least once while they're still fresh, and then once again before test review time.

The "Daily Assignment Sheet" (Diagram 3) is helpful in review, and good note-taking skills pay handsome dividends. If your teenager can read and understand his or her handwritten class notes and has completed assignments, the test should cause no trouble. And—even more important—

students have added useful subject matter to their mental
furnishings.

Ask for help if needed. The first commandment for
preparation is to understand the material to be tested.
When your teenager has never understood the material, going to the teacher for clarification is the obvious course.

You can offer your own help, of course. Or perhaps
another student or older brother or sister who has recently
taken the course can help clarify. And most schools can
supply lists of available tutors. The problem with these
other helpers is that they may have learned a different
system and, in trying to help, introduce terms and concepts
from their own system that only complicate things for the
already-troubled learner. Such confusion is particularly likely in subjects such as math or English grammar, where the
terminology and methods shift from one curriculum to
another or from one teacher to another.

The best advice: Get to the teacher.

If your teenager is reluctant (or refuses) to ask the
teacher, you may need to examine the tone of your own
interactions with your child, since teenagers often assume
that other adults are like their parents. If your teenager
seems reluctant to seek help in any class—no matter the
subject—you may find that, in honesty, you must answer
yes to one or more of these questions:

● Has your teenager learned from you never to question adult authority?

● Do you discourage questions in your household?

● When questions are asked, do you listen disrespect-
fully, not hearing the question out?

● Do you laugh or tease when your teenager admits
not knowing something?

● Do you run a "shut up and listen" household?

● Do you convey the impression that you (and therefore, presumably, all adults) know everything worth
knowing?

If your teenager's reluctance to ask for help applies to
only an occasional teacher, then something about that

teacher may be causing the reluctance. In that case, you and your teenager should think through options. You may decide together to seek another student's help or help from another teacher. Or you may decide together that your teenager has to muster the courage to approach the feared teacher. In some schools, you can ask the counselor to facilitate the student's contact with the teacher.

Approaching a teacher for help can be an intimidating experience—especially since teenagers are used to proving to the teacher what they *do* know. Admitting that they don't know something is difficult. If you can help your teenager figure out a comfortable approach, you're teaching a skill that will be useful throughout life.

Here's an approach that works for many students:

● In asking for help, it's both courteous and appropriate to take responsibility for having to ask. A student should never imply that it's the teacher's fault that the student doesn't understand, even though it may be. "I guess I just didn't get it when you were explaining . . ." is a good start.

● Clarify what you want. "I want to understand it before the test on Friday" explains when the teenager wants help, making it clear that next week isn't soon enough.

● Don't assume the teacher will drop everything else to sit right down for a tutoring session. Again, the student should take responsibility. "Could you tell me what I should do to get this straight?" or "Is there a time you could help me with this?" Approached in this way, most teachers will go out of their way to help.

Play being teacher. Encourage your teenager to think like a teacher at review time. Have him or her ask: If I were writing a test for my class, what would I ask? What kinds of things has this teacher asked about before? What did the teacher emphasize by saying things such as: "This is really important," or "You'll want to remember this"? Keep those things firmly in mind. Students are sometimes surprised to find how much they actually think like their teacher.

Come to test time rested. Students only hurt themselves when they let everything go until after dinner on the night before the test, cram in all the learning overnight, and retain what they learned just long enough to get through the test. This scenario happens much too frequently, and it represents the ultimate in grade-chasing without caring about the real learning the grade symbolizes.

Relax physically during the test. As hard as it is for students to relax when they're worried, relaxing physically occasionally while taking a test slows down the racing mind to a sane pace. Encourage your teenager to pause to look up now and then during the test. Take a few deep breaths. Tensing and then relaxing the arm, back and neck muscles make for a calming and mind-clearing break.

Pay attention. Some test-takers want to kick themselves later for answering a question entirely wrong because they didn't read the question properly. Your teenager can avoid such problems by paying attention to every word of the question. Most of the time when a student truly can't understand a question, asking for clarification is okay. Legitimate mistakes (the kind students make because they don't know the answer) happen often enough. Who needs the careless mistakes that result when they don't understand the question?

Do the easy stuff first. When students receive the test, they should first look through it quickly to see what's there. When they see something that's easy to answer, they should answer it first. If true-false and multiple choice questions seem easiest, start there. Save enough time later to come back to tussle with the tough ones. It's disastrous for a student to get stuck on a tough one so long that he or she doesn't have time to finish the test.

Answer with the first thing that seems right. Even if a student thinks of a different answer later, it's best to write down the first thought. There's time later for a personal debate over two different answers. But the first answer should get down on paper right away. Though the answer may not be right, statistics indicate that it often is.

Focus on the test. Concentration—which is not at all the same as tension—is essential. Students should sweep out of their minds such distractions as tomorrow's test or the babysitting job tonight with those impossible twins. The test is the only thing they can do anything about right now. The other worries will have to be taken care of later.

Don't start writing immediately on essay tests. Essay tests need lists and notes in the margin. Students should collect their thoughts about a question by scribbling in the margin a list of things they can say. With the list done, they can begin writing, using the list's clues and reminders about the topic.

Long-Term Benefits

Learning to study is a lot of trouble. But it's even more trouble not to know how. Without that knowledge, a person is permanently handicapped.

Another essential component lies beyond the specific skills: self-discipline. Screening out distractions and concentrating on a textbook is hard work. It's hard work to apply yourself to learning the difference between dependent and independent clauses or the proper way to add fractions.

However, a young person or an adult who hasn't learned self-discipline will never be free from the tyranny of the momentary wish or the fleeting impulse. Knowing how to learn and exerting the effort to do so is the only route, finally, to the freedom that mastering a subject, skill or process can bring. And there's no other way to exercise fully our stewardship of the unique identity that God has given each of us.

CHAPTER 8

Keeping in Touch With the School

"**D**on't tell him I called," Mrs. Berg pleaded on the phone. "He'd kill me if he knew. He doesn't want me to know anything about what happens at school!"

Even deducting a few points for hyperbole (few sons actually commit murder because of a phone call), we know things aren't as they should be at the Berg household. Mrs. Berg is a terrorized parent who urgently needs to understand—for her sake and her son's sake—that her appropriate role in her son's education involves being in touch with those who help that process along.

There's no need for a complete separation between school and home life for teenagers to achieve the independence they seek. What happens in each area affects behavior and feelings in the other. Keeping communication open facilitates a safe, warm, welcoming and productive environment for teenagers' living and learning.

Some parents mistakenly see themselves as adversaries to the schools. Just the opposite should be true. Both parents and educators are working for essentially the same results: for young people to get a sound education, operate according to school rules and regulations, and enjoy the school experience. Of course, you may differ with a teacher or administrator on particular points. But your mutual concern for your teenager's education should encourage you to

"Don't tell my daughter I came . . ."

keep in touch with educators.

Educators don't consider parents involved in school affairs to be intrusive. In fact, they welcome parents' interest. A Gallup Poll of public school teachers found that they believe the #1 impediment to education is "parents' lack of interest/support."[1] Providing young people with a high-quality education is so important to teachers that they've devoted their professional lives to it. They like having other people care about it too.

Let's discuss ways you can stay in touch with school. They include: phone calls, school visits, parent-teacher conferences, interim progress reports, newsletters and parent advisory groups.

 ## *P*hone *Calls*

Schools have phones for a purpose: to let people get in touch with what's going on at school. There are both routine and non-routine instances when a parent should contact the school. Often, a phone call is all that's necessary.

Teachers usually aren't available at the moment you call, but they will get in touch after school hours. If the call doesn't come, don't assume you're being purposely ignored. Human error sometimes accounts for lost call slips or forgetting. Call again.

Most schools have one or more counselors who can connect you with the appropriate person if you're not sure whom to call. Don't hesitate to call the school for fear of being thought overprotective. If school people think it's best for you to be patient while your teenager works out the problem alone, they'll tell you.

There are dozens of times when your routine call to your teenager's school is appropriate and expected. They include:

- Reporting your teenager's illness.
- Notifying school about a planned trip.
- Informing the office of a scheduled medical appoint-

ment during school hours.
- Asking about school vacation days.
- Inquiring when the track season starts.

Schools also welcome unusual information or special requests—although many parents hesitate to make such calls. Such calls may involve many different concerns, including rumors from school, teenagers' complaints, medical or personal needs, or a young person's anxieties about school.

Rumors. Puzzling things sometimes happen at school.

Though it seemed unbelievable, Mona Mackey swore it was true. She was leaving school after all the buses and most students had left, when: "I saw Mr. Anderson pushing somebody in a wheelchair, going real fast down the hall away from me. Then the person in the wheelchair dropped something and kind of slumped over—sort of fainted or something. And Mr. Anderson picked up whatever dropped and just kept going around the corner. He didn't even pay any attention to the *person!*"

Such callous treatment didn't seem characteristic to Mrs. Mackey, but the image kept bothering her. Finally, mid-morning the next day, she called the school. The principal's secretary wasn't aware that anyone was injured, but she agreed to investigate.

By noon she called back with the story: Mr. Anderson, who worked with gifted students, had been preparing for an "Odyssey of the Mind" competition. Since part of the competition involved using a wheelchair and another part required a dummy borrowed from the drama department, he had loaded the dummy and various other pieces of equipment onto the wheelchair for an efficient trip to his classroom.

Because Mrs. Mackey checked the story, the puzzle was solved, the secretary and Mrs. Mackey shared a chuckle, and Mrs. Mackey restored her confidence in the school's staff.

When your teenager comes home from school with a "screaming headline" story, it's always a good idea to check it out. School people gladly clarify to parents whatever puzzles them about school events.

Teenagers' complaints. Sometimes you need to check the details of a specific school situation before you jump to conclusions about it. Such is the case with teenagers' complaints about school. Often when you check out a story your teenager tells you, you hear another, equally logical side.

Pam's father wisely checked with her teacher on the accuracy of Pam's claim that "I'm behind in history, and we can't take the book home." With just a phone call, Pam's dad found that the teacher was quite willing for Pam to check out a text from the classroom set, provided she returned it before the following morning's classes.

Ninth-grader Howie told his dad that his teacher refused to give him credit for a metalwork project because it was late. "And only one day late too," Howie complained. Howie's father recognized the disappointment in his son's words, but he was also reluctant to believe the story was that simple.

So he called the teacher. He learned that when the teacher had assigned the project two weeks earlier, he had announced that the term's grades would be turned in to the office on Friday. Therefore, no project turned in later than Friday could be accepted for credit that term. At school—as at work—some deadlines are absolute. Howie's dad was right to look further for more of the story rather than accepting his teenager's story at face value.

Medical or personal needs. Your teenager may, at times, have medical or personal needs that appear to conflict with school rules or school expectations. Instead of fretting about the problem, call the school. Most teachers and administrators are willing to make special arrangements.

Joe's mother was concerned that Joe had to eat something along with his 10 a.m., noon and 2 p.m. medications through the week, but knew that school rules forbade eating at one's locker. The school made arrangements for the health aide to take custody of Joe's supply of snacks at her office, as well as the medication.

It also helps school staff to receive information about home life. If teachers know Sara is under stress because her father is undergoing major surgery, they can better interpret things Sara does that aren't characteristic of her—a lack of attention in class, for instance, or late assignments.

Anxieties about school. Jeremy's father reported that his sixth-grade son frequently said he was afraid to start junior high school because he heard that "kids get beat up there." Time for a broader perspective.

Jeremy's father called the school counselor. The counselor noted that when hundreds of 12- to 15-year-olds occupy and move about in the same building seven hours a day, 180 days a year, some physical conflict is inevitable. Educators expect this to happen, he explained, but that doesn't mean they tolerate it. When one student's behavior encroaches on others' rights, teachers and administrators monitor and correct it.

Hundreds of students experience happy, productive times at school, never encountering even a threat or shove. But if a minor scuffle does occur, the report will be issued with relish at 20 or 30 dinner tables that evening: "I heard that an eighth-grader beat up on a seventh-grader today." It's the kind of shocking news teenagers delight in feeding each other, embroidering and embellishing, and then throwing it into an otherwise calm (for the teenager, "boring") dinner conversation. In many cases, a call to the school can relieve any fears you might have.

Though the telephone is useful for many of your contacts with school, it isn't always the best instrument for the job. Sensing that little homework was being completed, Juanita's mother called the 10th-grade counselor on a Wednesday to ask if he'd check with Juanita's teachers on incomplete homework. The counselor sent notes to Juanita's five teachers asking for a report. On Thursday, three of the five had replied. By Friday all reports of missing assignments were in. The counselor telephoned the mother. The English teacher had noted the following:

-WS 23, 25, 26
-Measurement
-Outline Ex. 6

Neither the counselor nor the mother knew exactly what the notes meant, but they assumed Juanita would know. She did, and she explained when she came home Friday afternoon. But since she hadn't collected the information herself, she didn't bring home any of the materials to complete the missing assignments. That delayed any action until Monday night, and she wouldn't be able to turn in anything until Tuesday at the earliest—almost a week after the initial call requesting information.

Moral: Sometimes it's better to use more direct contact than the telephone to learn information. Often it's more efficient to have the teenager gather the information for you.

School Visits

Sometimes it's important to visit your teenager's school for a special in-person conversation with a teacher, counselor, coach or administrator. While these meetings can sometimes be difficult and awkward, they provide a valuable way for you and educators to work together to help your teenager.

Some parents find themselves particularly apprehensive about visiting their teenager's school. "I get butterflies in my stomach every time I step onto the schoolyard," Mrs. Arthur confessed. Dealing with their children's school is particularly difficult for parents like Mrs. Arthur, who dropped out after 10th grade and still carries vivid memories of her own unhappy school experiences. She desperately wants things to be better for her daughter.

If your own butterflies begin to flutter when you get near school, remember that courage isn't a matter of not being afraid; it's a matter of doing what needs to be done despite your anxiety.

One good way to ease the discomfort of visiting the school when your teenager has a problem is to stop by school occasionally—to drop off a forgotten musical instrument, to pay a football participation fee, or to attend a school event in the evening. Attendance at athletic events, awards ceremonies, concerts, dramatic productions, PTA meetings and open houses shows parental support and encouragement to your teenager. Such activities also help overcome some parents' feelings of being out of place when they visit schools.

There's also something reassuring about having a feel for the building where your teenager spends so much time—how it looks, how it sounds and smells in the corridors and classrooms. Then if your teenager comes home full of stories about school, you can visualize the setting far better and perhaps even understand the story's point more readily.

A visit may be necessary when your teenager feels wronged by a teacher. During a poetry unit in his sophomore English class, Mr. Wilkins asked students to write an original poem of at least eight lines. Judy—who had been getting mostly C's all year—turned in an exceptional poem. She had meticulously followed all the rules of meter and rhyme. The result was so outstanding that Mr. Wilkins questioned its authorship.

Judy reported her hallway encounter with Mr. Wilkins to her mother, who then phoned for an appointment with the teacher. Judy's mother explained that she had watched Judy struggle with the assignment the night before, and she knew the poem was original. In talking with the mother, Mr. Wilkins was quickly convinced that his suspicions were wrong. He apologized to Judy, and awarded her the A her poem deserved.

If school administrators or teachers ask for a meeting, give it high priority. Working parents often need to be creative to find a time to meet. Coaches and advisers for various other activities are often busy after school. Before-school appointments, when most staff members are available, are quite common. If your work schedule makes only a 7 a.m. meeting possible, school people will often accommodate you.

Despite occasional exceptions, it's usually better for your teenager to be present during school visits. Of course, he or she won't freely choose to participate—accurately anticipating some heavy discussion. But insist. If the teenager isn't there, how can you respond to your teenager's claim, back at home, that those three papers were in on time no matter what the teacher says? And unless the teenager is at the meeting, how can parents deal with their child's assurance that he or she never uttered the disrespectful words the teacher charges? Finally, having your teenager present to "face the music" directly increases the emotional impact and provides motivation to correct what's not going right.

Parent-Teacher Conferences

More and more junior and senior high schools now hold parent-teacher conferences once or twice a year. These provide important forums for parent-teacher dialogue.

Although the percentage of parents who attend these conferences gradually diminishes from the early grades up through high school, their importance doesn't decrease. No matter what your student's age, visiting school and talking with teachers underlines the high value you place on your teenager's education (which touches both your teenager's motivations and values). And, in our experience, these visits invariably deepen our understanding of and respect for the place where our children spend their days. It often increases our respect for the difficulty of the material the students are learning as well.

These conferences also have another important benefit: They allow you to talk with another adult who knows large numbers of young people your teenager's age. Their perspective can give you a helpful "big picture" view. The teacher can tell you a lot about how your 16-year-old compares with other 16-year-olds in self-discipline, maturity of behavior, respect for others and ability to take responsibil-

ity. While you needn't escalate comparisons into competition, an occasional reading-by-comparison is often
reassuring. Many years ago a neighbor confided that she'd
been quite critical of her 7-year-old son. "But since I've
taken on a Cub Scout group," she said, "I've learned what
other 7-year-old boys are like, and I find that Craig has improved tremendously!"

Parent-teacher conferences on the secondary level
commonly take one of two forms:

1. At some schools, parent and teenager sit down with
the homeroom teacher or adviser. Together they look at
written reports from other teachers.

2. At other schools, parents confer with each teacher
individually. Sometimes teachers receive parents in their
classrooms; other times, all teachers gather in the gym or
another large room where parents can move from teacher
to teacher as opportunity offers.

Each plan has advantages and disadvantages. The first
plan is quicker, but you don't have face-to-face contact with
your child's other half-dozen teachers. Moreover, you can't
get answers to some of your questions. Meeting teachers in
the gym is efficient, but you can't get the sense of the
classroom environment ("Michael sits right over there").
You don't see the "late assignment" basket or this week's
assignments posted on the board or "that beautiful land-
scape Jenny painted in acrylic."

If your school arranges for you to visit with all
teachers, keep your visits short, in deference to other
parents waiting. If you haven't really said or heard all you'd
like to in six to eight minutes, arrange for a follow-up visit
another day.

When you attend a parent-teacher conference, come
prepared. Ahead of time, recall and write down questions
about subject matter or classroom activities that have arisen
in conversation with your teenager. Tell teachers what you
know about your teenager's feelings about school or about
that subject. Ask about the teacher's perceptions of your
teenager's attitude to the subject matter, focus on tasks,

social behavior and classroom contributions.

Your role isn't simply to sit back and accept what you hear or register complaints without suggesting a solution. Sometimes your role as a parent is to educate the teacher about what you're most interested in. If your message is clearly and positively stated, it will make a difference.

For example, if you're particularly concerned that your teenager learns to treat others with respect, that goal certainly wouldn't conflict with what the teacher wants. Your assurance that you care about it, too, will probably nudge it higher on the teacher's agenda than it might otherwise have been.

Parent-teacher conferences are also appropriate settings for discussing concerns you have about school rules or regulations. Every institution that requires many people to work together in close quarters must have some agreed-on rules. Schools are no exception.

If you question the appropriateness of some school rules or regulations, ask an administrator or teacher about them. If the issue is important to you, see if you can get the rules changed. But until they are changed, support them. If you quickly side with your teenager who complains that "a rule like that is ridiculous," without knowing the situation or rationale, you undermine the student's sense of citizenship and responsibility. You also miss an opportunity to help your teenager develop self-discipline and respect for people and institutions.

With the parent-teacher conferences (as for when-things-go-wrong conferences), it's best for your teenager to be present. Both the affirmations and the "needs improvement" reports are appropriately delivered directly to the student, not through a parent.

While your input as a parent is usually helpful, there are times when your comments can do more harm than good. Here are some precautions:

● Your own years-ago school experience is rarely germane. Keep it out of the conversation. Teachers cringe when a parent—in the presence of the teenager—says: "I can't really blame him for the low grades in geometry. I had a lot of trouble with that myself." The student now feels complete freedom to get low grades in geometry. After all, he's been told that ability to learn geometry didn't come in his genes. As a result, he is unlikely to make a disciplined effort to discover his own capacities in the subject.

● Another damaging comment is the "I was no angel in high school, myself" story. Such an admission immediately justifies in the teenager's mind almost any disregard of school regulations or disturbance of classroom decorum.

Interim Progress Reports

Schools issue report cards at the end of fixed marking periods. But many parents would benefit from an interim report to gauge progress along the way. Some teachers address this need by issuing midterm reports for all students or for those doing unsatisfactory work. And more and more teachers have computers to help with grading, which makes issuing reports at shorter intervals relatively simple.

While it's important for parents to stay informed, some parents expect more communication about grades than teachers who deal with 150 or more students a day can reasonably be expected to handle.

Parents who actively participate in their teenagers' education and who have only their own children to be concerned about should take responsibility themselves to ask for interim information, rather than leaving the burden with the teacher. Mark your calendar at the point about halfway through the marking period, and telephone or write for the information you want.

Some teenagers have incredibly vague memories about whether they're up-to-date on all their assignments—especially for courses they dislike. If your inquires about incomplete assignments elicit only a vague, "I don't know . . . I don't think I have any," try making an interim report card like Diagram 4.

Write your note across the top of the page. Then down the left-hand side of the sheet list the subjects you want a report about—English, math, wood shop. Space them to give room for each teacher's response.

Ask your teenager to present the sheet to each teacher at the beginning of class and to pick it up at the end of each period to deliver to the next teacher. At the end of the day, your teenager should return with the accumulated reports in hand, along with any materials needed for the unfinished work.

This progress report system has several advantages: First, it is immediate. If all goes well, you get the report the same day you ask for it. Catch-up work can begin that same evening. Also, the student stays involved in the process, rather than observing from the sidelines. Not only is the request, traveling from class to class in Tom's hands, filled more immediately, but any questions Tom has (he was just *sure* he had handed in "WS 23") can be worked out on the spot with the teacher.

Of course, completing the form isn't likely to gladden any teenager's heart. "Come on, Mom. I can't do that. It's too embarrassing!" Assure Tom that you know it may be embarrassing, but that's the surest way you know to get the information, since he himself doesn't seem to know. Perhaps the pain of carrying a sheet from class to class will impress on Tom's mind two important pieces of information:

● His mother considers disciplined attention to schoolwork important enough to make a fuss about; and

● He'll probably avoid trouble in the future if he's more conscientious in his schoolwork.

Newsletters

Another way of keeping in touch with the school is through the school newsletter for parents (something different from the student newspaper—though this newspaper

Diagram 4
Interim Report Card

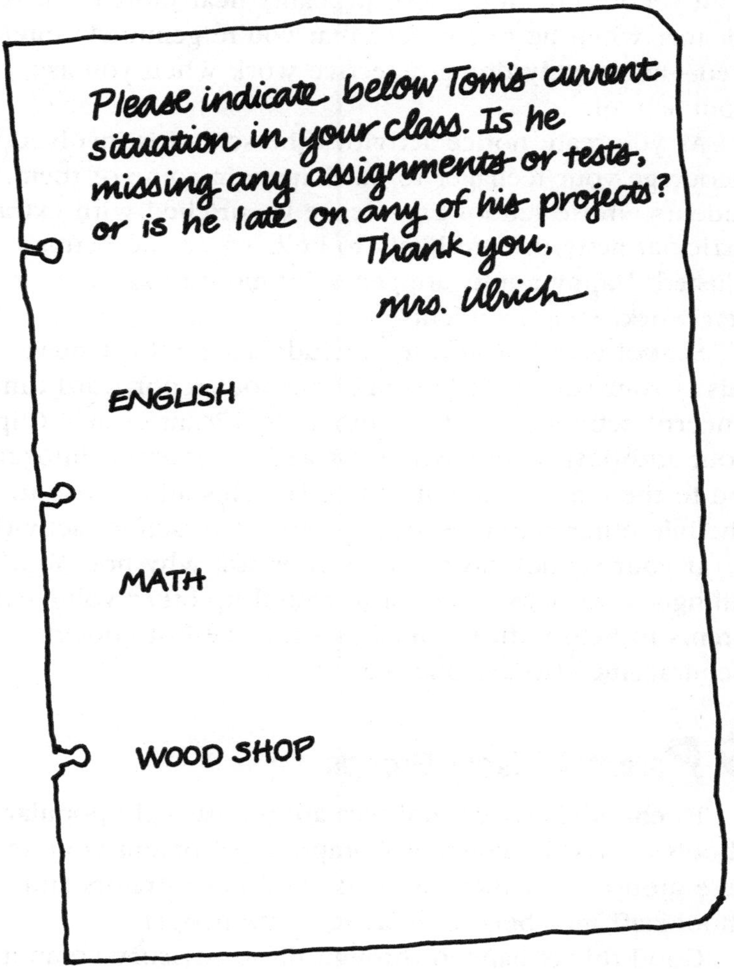

Please indicate below Tom's current situation in your class. Is he missing any assignments or tests, or is he late on any of his projects?
Thank you,
mrs. Ulrich

ENGLISH

MATH

WOOD SHOP

is informative too). Not all secondary schools issue such a newsletter, but many do.

If you have access to a school newsletter, read it thoroughly. It informs you about the range of school happenings, making it much easier to talk with your teenager about school life. You'll also probably hear more from your teenager when he or she sees that you're genuinely interested—not merely doing detective work when you ask about school.

As you read, notice activities the school is involved in. Encourage your teenager to participate in some of them. Students whose school experience is enriched with extracurricular activities are likely to be happier and better adjusted. Happy adults are generally more productive at their work. So are students.

School newsletters often include a school calendar. This is your source of information about report-card times, concerts, school parties and other significant events. Clip it out and post it somewhere, or add the relevant information to the family's activity calendar. This allows you to schedule other activities around important school activities.

If your school has no newsletter, ask why not. Your willingness to help—or even to round up other volunteer parents to help with the mailing—may be just enough encouragement to get one started.

🍎 *P*arent Advisory Groups

Parent advisory committees are increasingly popular in schools across the country. Composed of parent volunteers, these groups elect their own chairs. Administrators and school staff members serve as resource people.

Good things happen through these advisory committees. Parents discover they have power, when they thought they had none. They get first-hand information on what happens in the school, and why. And, perhaps most important, parents find they have influence in areas of school life—rules of behavior, selection of after-school activities and even the selection of some curricula.

Stories from around the country illustrate the impact you can have by participating in or starting such a parent advisory group:

● Parents at a junior high school were concerned about students' behavior at school parties. About 80 percent of the students attended the Friday-night parties, which were held three times a year and offered games, refreshments and dancing.

But problems had arisen. Some students with too many possessions and too little supervision were taking advantage of their parents' liquor cabinets between the end of the school day and party time. As a result, they arrived at the parties in various stages of tipsiness. Another problem involved enforcing the "students from this school only" rule, since high school students made a game of crashing the parties.

The parent advisory committee accepted the challenge. After much discussion, the committee members agreed that they could continue exactly the same activities for about the same length of time if they changed the time of the parties to after school. At this time, students were available, and they were much less vulnerable to the hazards of drinking or attracting older students.

After a slight initial flurry of resentment when party attendance dropped a bit, the afternoon custom is now firmly established, and attendance has returned to its former level. For several years now the relatively problem-free afternoon parties have provided the opportunity for excitement and socializing they were intended to provide—without the accompanying problems. And the students understood the logical progression of daytime elementary parties to after-school junior high parties to evening senior high parties.

● One spring, a Texas principal came to his parent advisory group with a curricular problem. Preregistration had revealed that introductory Spanish classes were filled to capacity, but introductory French and German classes would each have only about 10 students—not enough to justify hiring a teacher for each one. As a result, the school would have to drop the introductory courses.

But the parents weren't ready to let the matter rest. During the discussion an unexpected solution surfaced: Because the high school day began half an hour earlier than the junior high school's, junior high students could attend introductory French and German classes at the high school and a bus could then take them back to the junior high school in time for the next class. Problem solved.

● Parent advisory committees from two adjacent inner-city high schools met together to discuss the problem of summer "dead time" for students and schools. Together they discovered that, at a relatively low cost, the two schools could pool resources and facilities to offer summer courses in home economics, art, computer keyboarding, rocketry, drama and gardening. Teenagers, who'd otherwise spend the summer idle, unemployed and bored, quickly filled the special classes.

● In a small Southern town, the parent advisory committee approached the school with a concern. The local video game arcade—where many students spent their leisure time—had become a center for drug dealing. "It seems like that's the only place my daughter can meet her friends, and I'm worried about her being there," a father complained.

As a result of the concern, the school agreed to hold Friday evening activity nights twice a month, with volleyball, pingpong, swimming and computer games. The advisory group provided parental supervision. And a nominal fee allowed young people to meet in a relaxed and safe environment.

🍎 Working Together

As a parent, you may already be using some of these avenues of contact with teachers and administrators. You may also see some new ways to address your concerns.

Some of the ideas we've suggested may not fit your particular situation. Or you may have thought of other ways to maintain close contact.

Whatever methods you choose, remember that a parent has every right to contact schools, either to ask questions or to give information. Lack of contact deprives teenagers of the support that parents and school—working together—can give. Such contact can give you, as a parent, a better perspective on your child's education. It can also help teachers understand and work with your teenager.

 CHAPTER 9

What Do You Do When Nothing Works?

"**I**'ve tried everything I can think of, and nothing works!" Mr. Lytton exclaimed, his frustration evident even over the phone. The counselor's quick review of his son's first-quarter report card explained why. Mike's report card showed F's in biology and history, and several of his other grades weren't much better.

When a teenager fails to complete assignments, fails tests and makes no apparent effort to learn—and grades reveal those failures—what can parents do?

🍎 *The Limitations of Punishment*

Many parents in Mr. Lytton's situation do what he did: resort to obvious punishments. They ground their teenagers for a week or more, deny freedom to attend sports or other activities, withdraw telephone privileges, or forbid contact with friends. However, parents who try these methods rarely find that grades improve.

Outraged by the number of "assignments missing" and "homework not completed" notations on Mike's November report card, Mike's father exercised his parental power and forbade Mike to go out for his favorite sport, basketball. Surely *that* would make him attend to his daily work.

It didn't, of course. Mike resented the restriction so

much that he decided to "really *show* Dad." He did even less schoolwork. He knew his inaction would continue to keep him from playing basketball, but he had discovered that two can play the power game. And, at age 16, the only real power he had over his father was to get low grades. He knew they upset his father. Mike didn't give much thought to how his inaction could affect his chances for a college education. Future consequences came second to Mike's desire for a larger stake in his own life.

Mike's dad agreed to meet with the school counselor. After two discussions about teenagers' need to take more responsibility for themselves, Mike's father decided to admit his error and drop the ban on basketball practice. The counselor helped Mike and his dad negotiate the agreement: Mike would go out for basketball (partway into the season though it was) in exchange for setting a structured study time at home.

Mike played basketball, and his grades began to improve. Mike also saw his father in a new light—probably the best thing to come out of the entire story. Seeing his father's willingness to change, Mike learned that admitting a judgment error can be a real show of strength.

Part of the difficulty with the common punishments is that there's no clear link between the infraction and the punishment. Keeping Mike out of basketball practice between 3 and 5 p.m. doesn't lead dependably to study at that time. Study and basketball aren't in real conflict; there's time for both. Something else is going on between Mike and his dad. In order to address the problem, they had to dig beneath the behavior (poor school performance) to look at the student's motivation.

Similarly, denying telephone privileges usually increases resentment, but not study. And forbidding contact with a particular friend is virtually impossible when the two see each other daily in school. When parents impose such restrictions, the main results are hostile feelings toward the parent and more creative deception by the teenager.

Of course, denying telephone use during the scheduled

"I wish we could figure out some way to make Sarah concentrate on her homework."

Quiet Time for study is different. There's an obvious conflict between such interruptions and the goal. So someone else should answer the phone and take messages during that time.

Ways Parents Respond to Problems

Parents respond in different ways when grades decline. Some are healthy; others are not. Parental action with teenagers when grades go bad usually falls into one of three types:

Authoritarian. The authoritarian says: "I will decide. You will do." This power play rarely improves grades, and it nearly always generates resentment. This method appears to work for some parents during elementary years and, too often, they assume it will continue to work in secondary school. But the fear that helped it work in elementary school has lost some of its power, and the aggrieved and puzzled parent reports: "She always obeyed me up until now. I can't understand what's happened to her."

During adolescence teenagers are searching for identity. Becoming a separate "me" is a high priority. As a result, authoritarian parents encounter real problems. Many parents find that their child knows about and can exercise the power of passive resistance. They're dismayed to find that the old controlling methods have stopped working, and they have no idea what else to try.

Permissive. Occupying the opposite end of the control scale from the authoritarian is the permissive parenting style. Parents who apply this method allow their teenagers almost unlimited freedom to express themselves.

Without any defined behavior guidelines, these teenagers find a freedom that feels delightful at first. They can do their own thing without feeling compelled to take any responsibility—either in school or out. Eventually, however, teenagers find that this kind of "freedom" carries a price. Sooner or later, most of these teenagers develop a strong suspicion that their parents don't really care enough about them to set and enforce the kinds of limits that their friends' parents provide. And they resent being deprived of that evidence of caring.

Democratic. The third type of control—which falls between the authoritarian and the permissive—is a more democratic, give-and-take relationship between teenager and parent. These parents don't relinquish all control, but they allow their teenagers to make choices within set parameters. They may say:

● "You may not participate in more than two activities other than your school classes. But you may choose which activities they will be."

● "You must join us in Quiet Time for one hour on school nights. You can decide what to study or read, and we'll work toward family agreement on when it will be scheduled."

This parenting style promotes harmony rather than conflict. Teenagers in these families can state preferences and be heard (great inducements to cooperation). These teenagers know they are regarded as significant, and they feel respected and loved.

The democratic parenting style offers the best response to school problems. For example, when a routine has been set up but isn't working, parent and teenager together should evaluate it and analyze any flaws in the plan. To help keep accusations out of the process, discuss the plan as if it had been set up *by* someone else *for* someone else. Don't say, "You should have known I can't . . ." Instead, you could say, "The plan doesn't allow for a different schedule on Wednesday and Friday." Express your concerns as respectfully as you would with another adult or fellow worker.

Ask your teenager for his or her opinion on why the plan isn't working. Wait out the usual "I don't know" for a meaningful answer. Don't be too quick with your insightful parental analysis. List the possible adjustments in the plan and try to come to a mutual agreement on the changes needed. Agree that the new plan is experimental, and check how it's going in another parent-teenager discussion in a couple of weeks.

Dealing With a Learning Disability

In the past decade or two, we've become more aware of the great variety of genuine learning disabilities. Particular anomalies in the physical or neurological makeup of individual children interfere with the complicated process of taking in, organizing and remembering information. Sophisticated diagnostic and treatment methods are available, and federal regulations require schools to provide separate educational programs for students who have such problems.

If, after various attempts to help have failed, you're baffled by your teenager's lack of school success, you may want to talk with a teacher or counselor about finding out whether a learning disability is present. Having special educational help now has less of a stigma than it used to. More and more students receive special help as assessment and treatment become more refined and as more students come to understand that receiving help is better than floundering in the mainstream classroom.

Parents owe it to teenagers who are encountering serious school problems to find out whether those problems are the result of something entirely beyond the student's control. If the assessment team finds no evidence of a disability, counselors will tell you so. If one is found, the school's team should invite you to be involved in designing a program to deal with the problem, either by compensating for the disability or finding a remedy.

The length of time needed for special educational help varies with the student and the type of disability. No matter the duration, parents continue to be part of the periodic review. By law, as soon as a less restrictive alternative is possible, the treatment will end and the student will return to the mainstream classroom. In fact, most students with learning disabilities never leave the mainstream classroom for most of their classes. They get help only in those areas of greatest need.

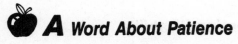

A *Word About Patience*

A doctor friend says that he thinks as many as 75 percent of his patients—if left to their body's own resources—would recover from their illness without diagnosis or professional treatment. It might take them much longer to get well, of course, but they would get well.

A similar claim could be made about some teenagers' educational ailments. Some school problems work themselves out with time and the teenager's own inner resources. Most people whose children have moved into adulthood will assure you that many of the "crazies" of the teenage years eventually disappear. Parents need patience. Much of the turbulence of young adolescence works itself out by the passing of time.

However, to caution patience with your teenager doesn't mean you should do nothing. This perspective doesn't suggest ignoring either medical or educational symptoms. In both instances, early treatment usually is most effective. Parents need to take whatever reasonable action they can to correct school-related problems. But they must also be patient and ride out the storm.

If you're trying to deal with an entrenched school problem, think about the whole child and about the four levels of reality discussed in Chapter 3. When new and puzzling behaviors appear, look deeper at possible motivations, possible fears. Discuss the importance of education for you. Talk about what your teenager sees as the purpose of his or her education—what goals lie ahead.

Beware of making too much of a single out-of-character incident or a way of dressing or acting that you find distasteful. A coughing spell doesn't always indicate the onset of pneumonia. One report card doesn't reflect the whole person. One act of dishonesty, while it's certainly not something you let slip without comment, doesn't reflect the whole person. One incident of blatant disrespect doesn't reflect the whole person. Perhaps we can be more patient when we remember that some of the troubling behaviors will disappear by themselves.

Parents eagerly want their children to reach the full potential God has built into them, and so concerned parents worry when their child seems to be wasting his or her time and educational opportunity. But sometimes they jump too early into the picture with an action plan. Concerned parents are wonderful, but sometimes their dismay and quick reaction get in their teenager's way. In the long run, a calm and thoughtful approach is much more likely to succeed.

Many highly successful and productive adults look back ruefully at a year or two of disastrous grades or behavior in secondary school. While those adults wouldn't suggest that parents adopt a "let's wait and see" attitude about the problems, they do know how rapidly a teenager can catch up. Many of the problems fade as the teenager develops a more certain sense of identity and the more mature values that accompany it.

Seeking Outside Help

Some teenagers continue not to achieve at their level of potential. And they continue to fail despite conversations, plans and routines. These young people need special attention. In order to get to the root of the problem, that attention must sometimes extend to their parents as well.

At times, school problems grow out of problems in the parent-teenager relationship. Sometimes the teenager does poorly in order to get a parent's attention. Sometimes he or she needs to emphasize a sense of identity separate from parents. And sometimes poor grades are used to "get back" at parents for some real or imagined wrong.

It happens.

Tony was an eighth-grader with an IQ of 145. His younger brother was a happy, popular fifth-grader. The family was active in the church where his mother was an organist.

Tony's father, an engineer, was an intelligent, disciplined man who liked things organized and hierarchical. He made the family rules and insisted they be followed. The mother usually waited patiently to discover what her husband had decided, then agreed.

Through sixth grade, Tony excelled in all his schoolwork. But then in seventh grade, things began to slip. By eighth grade his school performance hit bottom.

After weeks of school counseling, Tony confided in the counselor: "I've tried everything to get them to stop bossing me around. I've tried arguing with them. I've tried running around with the crummiest kids in school. But the one thing that really gets them is grades. Grades are *so* important to both of them. And now I've got 'em. They can't *make* me study or get better grades."

Tony flunked eighth grade. And he was right: The failure got his parents' attention. They felt deeply embarrassed and humiliated before their friends. Despite the father's extreme reservations, they finally agreed to enter family counseling. In the counseling process, they learned together as a family that it was impossible to exercise complete control over one another's actions. And they learned how to communicate their wants in more positive and constructive ways.

Tony repeated eighth grade, doing only a little better than he had the first time around. But in senior high, at last, he began to blossom academically. He qualified for an academic scholarship that got him well on his way to college work.

It's sometimes difficult for us to see what's going on in our families until we're willing to "let in" a professional counselor who can observe the family dynamics and tell us what he or she sees. A set of nose-diving grades is often symptomatic of a deeper problem that involves the dynamics of the whole family. Sending an underachieving young person off to a therapist alone to "get fixed" almost never addresses the root cause.

In order to look successfully at the deeper levels of motivation, value and identity that drive each family member, we must sometimes invite a trained, outside person to help. The crucial questions for both parent and teenager then become:

● Why are grades and school success so important to me?

● What do they symbolize for me?

● How can I expand my understanding so we can resolve the conflicts between me and the rest of the family?

What parents need most in these difficult situations is to exercise humility—that quality so central in the Christian life and parenthood. We must be prepared to admit that we don't know everything. And we must be willing to accept the advice and ministry of one who can look at us with an outsider's insight and show us the way to become whole as a family again.

CHAPTER 10

Conflicts With School—
Real and Imagined

Today's teenagers are busier than ever. They have more freedom, more opportunities, more responsibilities than ever before. Many are like Anita, who—in addition to classwork—plays flute in the marching band, serves on the student council, is president of the youth group at church, holds a steady job at the mall and spends a couple of evenings a week with her boyfriend. She's always busy, and her drivers license gives her the freedom to set her own schedule and go places when she needs or wants to.

As parents, we sometimes wonder whether all this activity is really good for our teenagers. And we worry that it might all be interfering with their education. On the other hand, we know that these activities are an important part of growing up. How can we tell the difference? Where do we need to give our teenagers guidance and direction?

In this chapter we'll look at four different areas of life that sometimes seem to conflict with schoolwork: part-time jobs, extracurricular activities, social life and household chores. We'll examine whether they do indeed interfere, and how we as parents can work with our teenagers to set boundaries to keep their lives in balance.

🍎 *Part-Time Jobs*

A generation or two ago people rarely even asked whether high school students should hold part-time jobs during the school year. If a teenager worked during high school, it was because the parents needed help on the farm, the family needed the added income, or the young person was saving for college expenses.

But now the picture has changed. Teenagers from middle-class and affluent neighborhoods alike turn up all over the place, serving up burgers, checking out groceries and selling everything from dog food to earrings in the shopping malls.

The statistics confirm the change we observe. The U.S. Bureau of Labor Statistics reports that in 1947, 27 percent of boys aged 14 to 17 worked. In 1980, 44 percent had jobs. Over the same period, the figure for girls rose from 17 to 41 percent.[1] And the percentages are still rising. According to a 1986 Indiana University-Phi Delta Kappa study, 70 percent of high school seniors held paid jobs during the school year.[2]

Working part time while going to school is obviously common among high school students. But what is it doing to their education? Is it a good idea? There is no simple answer. There are both pros and cons to having a job during the high school years, and the fact that so many students are joining the work force doesn't mean that the trend is wise or best for them.

Benefits. The arguments *for* working are easy to see:

1. Productive use of spare time. Parents know that work expands to fill the time available. John's parents have seen their son stretch what should be a 20-minute homework assignment into an entire evening's occupation. With the trips to the refrigerator, a phone call or two, a break to see a "must" TV show and a routine spat with a younger brother, it's no wonder John thinks it took him the whole evening to do the assignment. His parents can be pardoned for thinking a job might be a good replacement for all that leisurely time-filling. Perhaps, they think, it would teach him self-discipline too.

2. Adult responsibility. Teenagers with long records of absentmindedness about mailing letters and feeding dogs tend to improve wonderfully when they're given a list of tasks in a work-for-pay setting. Further, a 16-year-old who must balance out cash receipts at the end of the day and see that they are properly recorded and deposited is learning something about taking responsibility seriously.

3. Independence. The independence that comes from having money of their own is attractive to teenagers. Parents affirm, "It's important for a young person to learn to handle money."

4. Understanding the work place. Working part time helps teenagers understand the realities of the work place. They see that jobs differ. Routine and mind-numbing jobs have convinced many teenagers that continuing their education will earn them more interesting work. "I'd hate to do *this* for the rest of my life."

Dangers. But there are also some fairly serious indications that working during the school year also endangers some important values:

1. Interference with education. In general, teenagers who work find that it interferes with the educational process. Work often usurps the time that should be spent studying and preparing to make the best use of class time and teacher expertise. So working students often don't complete homework and don't finish reading assignments that prepare them for class.

As a result, some critics of teenagers' working charge, teachers eventually "dumb down" a course because they've been confronted so often with students who show ignorance of terms or concepts that were amply explained in the assigned reading. In these cases, teachers end up reducing time for the more appropriate and sophisticated discussion, replacing it with the elementary activity of reviewing the major points in the assigned reading. Moreover, some students attend class so tired from their late-night jobs that they doze off in the classroom.

2. Lower grades. Working part time often leads to lower grades. Each day has a finite number of hours, and time spent working is not spent studying. Research shows that senior boys who have jobs have lower grade point averages than their classmates who don't work.[3] Statistics also indicate that grades go down when the number of hours worked increases. Yet teenagers are strongly tempted to add more hours for more money.

3. Attitude toward education. Not only does working interfere with day-to-day learning, but it also may gradually influence students' attitudes about education. Interest in their work—or in the things their earnings buy—sometimes leads students to wonder, "If I can make the money I'm making now with what I know, what's so important about learning more?" Unfortunately, the answer to the "What's so important?" question may not become apparent until the young person has achieved an age and family situation that make it difficult to repair the wasted opportunity.

4. Premature affluence. But perhaps the most serious negative effect of part-time work on high school students is its introduction of what Ellen Greenberger and Laurence Steinberg call "premature affluence" in their book *When Teenagers Work: The Psychological and Social Costs of Adolescent Employment.* Most working students spend much or all of their earnings at their own discretion. In most homes, somebody else still covers the house payments and insurance, and buys the groceries, soap and paper towels. As a result, the student can spend his or her earnings on luxuries—impulse purchases, fad clothing, expensive dates and compact discs. About 75 percent of seniors surveyed say they only save "a little" or "none" of their earnings for future education, and more than 70 percent save only "a little" or "none" for long-range purposes.[4]

The results of such easy, impulsive buying are an "easy come, easy go" materialism, a cynical attitude toward work and, in some situations, an increased tolerance of unethical practices in business.[5] All of this breaks down the traits

Christian parents hope their children will develop—a sense of responsible stewardship of all of Earth's goods, a respect for honesty and a generosity of spirit.

When work is appropriate. With all these dangers of working part time, should any teenagers work during the school year? We think paid part-time work is desirable for a high school student in three situations:

1. Family support. Some teenagers must work to contribute to family support. University of Michigan research reveals that while 24 percent of black teenagers contribute half or more of their earnings to support their families, only 6 percent of white students help that much with family support.[6] The difference no doubt reflects the fact that many black families live near or below the poverty line.

2. Exploring a vocation. When a job is closely related to the kind of work the teenager wants to do as an adult (including a family business such as farming), the part-time job may be extremely beneficial. Such work can serve as an appropriate apprenticeship for a future vocation.

3. Saving for education. A third reason that justifies work during high school is to save the earnings for something related to education. Here are some activities we think qualify:

● Tuition to a music camp, computer camp and the like

● A church mission trip or camp

● Educational travel

● Tuition for college or other post-high school education

4. Summer jobs. Working during the summer break often provides the benefits of work during adolescence without most of the dangers of working during the school year.

Keeping perspective. Whether or not a teenager works, remember that school is a teenager's main job. Anything that interferes with schoolwork, therefore, is suspect. Adolescence is the time to devote to the tasks of education and growing up—not a time for hurrying to become a money machine.

A few hours of part-time work during high school in order to make some spending money probably doesn't hurt most students. But parents should raise serious questions about any job that involves more than 10 to 15 hours a week. Parents and teenagers should talk about whether the work will be helpful to the overall purposes of the teenager's education. Until the question is satisfactorily resolved, rushing into the work force may be a mistake.

*E*xtracurricular Activities

Parents sometimes make the mistake of suggesting that teenagers drop all extracurricular activities the moment their teenagers encounter any difficulty with schoolwork. That's too bad. Extracurricular activities add too many positive features to a student's total education to be considered mere frosting on the educational cake. They're different in several ways from courses in the regular curriculum, and they enhance any student's education in a variety of ways.

New opportunities for social interaction. Many after-school activities allow students to work together in small groups. In these groups young people come to understand, exchange ideas with and learn from fellow students. They develop new friendships. In an atmosphere less (or differently) structured than the classroom, they develop new relating skills and new ways to approach a given task.

Freedom and creativity. One of our elder daughter's best-remembered high school experiences followed her German class's decision to build a float for the homecoming parade. With no adult to supervise, the high schoolers were on their own.

Those 10 construction days were crammed full of logistical problems these youngsters had never met before. They learned a great deal about the properties of chicken wire and crepe paper, and the practical techniques of keeping bulky objects upright while in motion.

Day after day they faced problems and invented solutions with feverish intensity. In the process they developed increased respect for their own problem-solving skills, learned about exchanging roles as leader and follower as work demanded, and gained self-confidence. They also became fast friends. Fifteen years later, Beth still identifies high school friends by saying, "He built the float with us."

Opportunities to shine. Many a youngster who spends classroom time back in the pack somewhere—never at the head of the race—discovers and can display talents that bring status and a sense of self-worth. Such discovery happens a lot in extracurricular sports. It also happens in music, when quiet little Becky wins the regional music contest with her clarinet solo. And it happens in dramatic productions, when Juan plays a part that reveals an until-then hidden facet of his personality.

Once-in-a-lifetime opportunities. The number and variety of opportunities offered in junior and senior high school activities never appears again. To be sure, college has its share of extracurricular offerings too. But in college the stakes on academic achievement are even higher than in high school—and the competition's tougher. Many teenagers who played leads in their high school musicals are lucky to land a walk-on part in college. Work on the school newspaper in high school teaches many basic disciplines of news writing, but getting on the staff of a college paper is tough—and the hours are long. Better to master the basic techniques in high school.

Avoiding excess. As you can see, we strongly favor every student taking advantage of some high school extracurricular opportunities. However, there's a need for caution. Many students don't know when enough is enough. They need parents' help.

We know a number of youngsters who—in their enthusiasm for this smorgasbord of attractive possibilities—have filled their plates too full. Some could admit, partway into the term, that their promises had overtaxed their capacities.

"I work Tuesday. There's play practice Wednesday, followed by Stamp Club. Then we have band concerts Thursday, Friday and Saturday . . . It looks like I have 10 minutes to study for the English test next Monday."

They then made some hard choices of what to drop and what to keep. Others, less willing to make that admission, have run their frantic schedule to the point of severe physical illness which, of course, brought everything— academic work and all—to a halt.

In the same way parents prevent their teenagers from other overindulgences, they should try to prevent overindulgence in extracurricular activities. Adults have had more practice than teenagers at thinking ahead and estimating probable costs in time and energy. Those probable costs can be examined together with your teenager in the same way you might lay out a family budget. This approach lets the teenager pick and choose rationally, rather than trying everything at once and suffering the disappointment of certain eventual overload.

Some activities become all-consuming for brief periods of time, but you can usually predict and prepare for those periods. Float-building, for example, absorbs every spare minute for 10 days or more. A play can demand that the cast and crew attend rehearsals every week night and on weekends for two weeks before the performance. Similarly, dance and music contests usually demand increased rehearsal time.

Parents can help their teenagers anticipate these time crunches and plan ahead. A family may decide to cooperate by taking over the crunched member's household chores for a while or help with extra transportation. The extra effort and cooperation usually pay off in what the teenager gains in experience, sense of accomplishment, self-confidence, friendships and treasured memories.

Social Life

Learning how to get along with other people without adult supervision is a major learning of adolescence. The close supervision of childhood gives way to long stretches of time when teenagers interact without having adults around. This interaction gives young people an arena to try out what they've learned from their parents about "getting along." They find out whether those patterns really work or whether other ways work better. They try different roles: clown, listener, leader, follower—and they employ different styles—argumentative, supportive, cooperative, combative. They find out what works for them—and what doesn't.

Teenagers need to be able to plan activities together, to spend time in one another's homes, to talk, to invent teenage craziness, to amuse one another into helpless laughter and to "hang out." They need time for play, conversation, goofing off, speculating about the future, building air castles. Gina's problem wasn't her interest in other people and in what they thought of her. Those are normal. Her problem was that she let it take over the whole show.

If a student's interest in social life threatens to dominate other areas of life, parents need to intervene. In terms of the teenager's healthy social and academic growth, it doesn't matter much whether the social "unit" absorbing too much time is a member of the opposite sex, a member of the same sex, or a bunch of friends. In all such cases, parents best serve their teenager's interests by setting limits on the number and frequency of social interactions— telephone calls, trips to the mall, "cruising" or dating. As with any good thing (and friendships are, indeed, good things), friendships can become problems when they're overdone.

🍎 *Household Chores*

"I just can't understand why she doesn't do her homework," Mrs. Morris complained. "She has plenty of time. We don't require her to do anything around the house except keep her room picked up."

Despite her good intentions, Mrs. Morris isn't really helping Nancy achieve in school by relieving her of all household responsibilities. While other areas of life sometimes appear to interfere significantly with schoolwork, chores really don't. More than 30 years of work with students provides ample evidence that successful students are generally the same young people who take responsibility for home chores.

Excusing a teenager from all household chores in the hope that he or she will use the extra time to study doesn't work. In general, students who take responsibility at home are also responsible about schoolwork. In this case, having enough time is mostly a matter of knowing how to organize time. It's often the popular and active student who calls down the school hallway on Friday afternoon: "I'll get over to your place Saturday as soon as I can, but I gotta clean my room and the kitchen fridge first."

The importance of chores. An important part of teenagers' sense of identity is their knowledge of what they've done—now and in the past. If parents don't require their children to participate in housework and don't encourage participation in volunteer projects, they in effect cut off their teenagers from effective ways of developing a personal history that answers the questions, "Who am I?" and "Do I matter?" In addition, if we don't teach them how and why household chores should be done, we rob them of important life skills.

In the short term, a teenager probably thinks not doing chores is great. Everyone likes to escape work. But in the long term, the effect is loss, not gain. The teenager feels no sense of accomplishment, no sense of having contributed to the good of the family or any member of it. Sharing family responsibilities contributes to teenagers' sense of identity. They know they have successfully completed a difficult task, and they know they have done something useful for others.

Sharing chores. Every household member should help with some home chores. Negotiate guidelines and regulations for those chores among family members in the same fashion as Quiet Time in Chapter 7.

One approach for arranging family chores is to list the dozen or so tasks around the house that need doing regularly. Let family members each choose the ones they are willing to take on. If the process gets stalled in arguments, find a way to give everyone a fair chance at getting the job he or she wants. Pick a number between 1 and 100, and write it down. The person who guesses closest to that number begins, choosing one task. Then move to the left around the circle—and again around until all the jobs have been assigned.

The Wilson family—whose children range from 4 to 17—divide home chores into two categories: one set for those under age 10, and the other for those 10 and older. The older children have the hazardous jobs—mowing the lawn and running the snow blower, for instance. The less hazardous and less physically taxing jobs—setting the table or dusting the living room—were reserved for the younger children.

A posted assignment sheet reminds everyone who does what and when. A weekly or monthly rotation of tasks or trading off not only provides variety, but teaches cooperative negotiation. A young person who grows up sharing home chores is much more likely to take on easily the independent responsibility of keeping up with schoolwork.

Keeping Balance

The key word in dealing with these potential conflicts with school is balance. Some teenagers find room in their lives for successful academic work, occasional part-time jobs, a reasonable social life and selected extracurricular activities—if they manage their time well, and if they keep everything in balance.

Parents shouldn't advise their teenager to cut off everything but school. You can be most helpful by encouraging your teenager to think ahead and plan a reasonable amount of time for each activity. The resulting combination will contribute richly to the teenager's growth, learning and enjoyment of life.

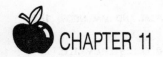 CHAPTER 11

Church and School: Working Together

A teenager's religious training and conviction don't become irrelevant at the edge of school property. At school, teenagers meet other teenagers whose religious faith and practice differ from their own, and they exchange private questions and private answers. These questions and efforts to answer are particularly important during adolescence when most young people raise questions and make judgments about their own religious tradition. As a result, young people may hear and discuss issues or opinions at school that conflict with the values they learn at home.

This practical challenge to their faith is another good reason conversations about school at home shouldn't stop with, "What time do you expect to be home?" and "Are you sure you want to wear *that* to school?" They need to include deeper, more reflective exchanges.

Conversations about faith and values offer two benefits to families: You and your teenager both learn as you talk, and your teenager finds out that it's possible to talk about values and beliefs at home. This openness gives teenagers a secure feeling that they can discuss their concerns openly when they run into a difficult question at school.

Jim liked his 11th-grade social studies teacher a lot. Mr. Abels was a good storyteller, and he made the class so interesting that Jim found himself looking forward to it every day. He had even given a little thought to being a social studies teacher himself someday.

But about the middle of the year, Jim became aware that the way Mr. Abels talked about national defense directly contradicted what Jim's parents believed about war as well as the tone and focus of his church youth group's discussions on the topic.

Jim knew his parents believed our country has, in recent history, relied too heavily on military strength, spending wealth on military hardware that would be better spent feeding, educating and protecting those who are hungry and in need.

In contrast to Jim's parents, Mr. Abels discussed the United States' position as a world leader, and the importance of holding that position through military strength. He spoke convincingly and seriously, and he clearly believed what he said.

Over a period of weeks, Jim became more and more uncertain of what he believed. Finally he told his parents about the conflict between their beliefs and Mr. Abels', and the choices he was struggling with.

His father nodded. "A lot of people in this country believe what Mr. Abels is saying," he said. "And a lot of people in this country also believe what Mom and I do. Has anybody in class mentioned the arguments in favor of reducing military expenditures?"

Jim remembered some students had, at first. "But," he said, "Mr. Abels knows so much more than we do. After a while nobody can think of anything else to say. So he just talks now, and we listen."

Jim's father pointed out that Mr. Abels' knowledge of social studies facts didn't guarantee his opinions were right. "I think there must be others in your class who are trying to work out the same puzzle you are. If you don't mind, I think I'll talk with your teacher."

Students of Jim's age often shrink from looking protected by their parents but, to his credit, Jim agreed.

Mr. Abels was at first surprised, and then apologetic. "I

suppose I get carried away sometimes," he confessed. He strongly believed in his position, but he also was aware that his position wasn't the only one taken by people in the community. "You're right," he said. "I should be presenting more for the other side of the issue. Do you know of any useful resources?"

Jim's father combined some of his own books with resources recommended by his denomination's state headquarters. Mr. Abels subsequently used the materials in a class presentation. He also began encouraging students to express their own beliefs more. Jim found that his hunch was right: About half the students in his class were more interested in spending government funds to take care of people than to increase defense spending.

There are many complex world and social issues over which thoughtful people disagree. When these issues arise in English, science, history or health classes, diverse opinions are inevitable—even among committed Christians. Public school teachers can't and shouldn't be expected to promote a particular perspective over others; they should be sensitive, fair and balanced when honest differences over controversial issues arise.

Value differences don't always end as harmoniously as the incident between Jim and Mr. Abels. But nothing will change unless you raise the questions. When what your teenager hears at school consistently opposes your family's values, try taking the following steps:

1. First see whether your teenager is willing to raise the issue with the teacher to try to get a hearing for opposing views.

2. If your teenager is unsuccessful, contact the teacher involved yourself.

3. If the situation is still unresolved, talk to the principal.

Public schools are expressions of community concern for education and are operated on community funds. Schools allow teachers a great deal of latitude in teaching style and grading policy. But teachers shouldn't be permitted, unchallenged, to present a one-sided view of a controversial topic in the community.

On the other hand, teachers must present a prescribed body of factual information, even if you would prefer that some of it not be included.

In presenting a unit on human sexuality, June's health teacher showed a film presenting a variety of birth-control methods. June had learned in her religious education classes at church that the Roman Catholic Church recognizes the use of only "natural" birth-control methods. Using some of the devices discussed in class (the condom, diaphragm, birth-control pill) was outside church teaching.

Like Jim, June told her parents about the presentation. And like Jim's parents, June's parents called the teacher. The teacher pointed out that presentation of all birth-control methods—including those defined in some religious faiths as artificial—was part of the regular curriculum. It was part of the information that had to be presented to the class. "I did forget, though," the teacher confessed, "to point out that some of the methods (and I usually say which ones) are outside church teaching for some students. I'm sorry I failed to do that. I'll fix that omission when we review the unit."

June's parents, of course, would have preferred that the artificial methods not be mentioned in the class at all. They took their question to the principal, who reminded them that their daughter was receiving public education along with children from homes with values that differed from theirs. "Certain factual matters that some parents want presented cannot be left out because of other parents' objections. The best I can do for you is to excuse your daughter from parts of the health curriculum that conflict with your wishes."

What is appropriate and inappropriate in schools? The U.S. Supreme Court has generally affirmed the appropriateness "of teaching *about* religion, as distinguished from the teaching *of* religion, in the public schools."[1] The Baptist Joint Committee on Public Affairs in Washington, D.C., lists the following examples based on U.S. Supreme Court decisions:

● The school can't insist that students recite official prayers.

● The school can't oppose or show hostility to religion, thus preferring non-believers over believers.

● State- or school-sponsored prayers or Bible readings are not appropriate.

● The Bible may be used as a reference for teaching secular subjects. It may also be studied for its literary and historic qualities.

● Public school students may study history of religions, comparative religions and the role of religion in the advancement of civilization.

● Schools may ask students to recite historical documents that contain references to God.[2]

 ## *Church-School Cooperation*

Religious practice and public education don't always conflict. In many communities, churches and schools have found ways to cooperate, and both teenagers and their families benefit. Each institution plays a unique role, but often their interests overlap or complement each other. Parents can be the catalysts for bringing church and school together to help their teenagers.

Churches and schools share many concerns. For example, schools constantly combat drug abuse among students. A major Search Institute study of drug use among students in Minnesota public schools (with results closely paralleled in a later study in Colorado) found a strong link between church activity and rejection of drug use.[3] Three of the top four items related to non-use of drugs were:

● Participation in religious youth programs

● Frequent worship attendance

● Religion as an important influence in the student's life

While their purposes are different, churches and

schools share some common goals. The two can work together in many areas without overstepping their appropriate roles. Not only does such cooperation reduce conflicts, but it also demonstrates each institution's respect for the other's activities. By encouraging the two organizations to work together, parents can have a positive impact on their child's development.

Here are some ways churches and schools can cooperate:

Arrange a church night. Schools in many communities work with the local ministerial association to define a "church night." The schools don't plan activities on these nights, allowing young people to participate in midweek services, choir practices, youth programs and confirmation preparation. Some teachers recognize church night by lightening the homework load a bit, or by allowing a day's leeway in homework deadlines that night.

If your community doesn't have such a designated time, maybe it's because no parents have asked for it. If yours is a one-school community, talk with the principal. Work with the school board in larger districts. If your church's youth come from several districts, the negotiation will be more complicated. But if you can save teenagers from the hard choices they otherwise have to make between church and school activities, the effort will be worth it.

Coordinate calendars. Be sure your church staff has and uses the school calendar. A three-day church-related ski trip is a real headache for teachers if it comes during a term's final week.

At the same time, many school systems have school in-service training days and other one-day scheduled breaks that involve teachers but not students. These are ideal for planning youth trips and other church activities.

Exchange information. Church youth workers and school people can be helpful resources to one another. Some communities arrange annual meetings of pastors, school counselors, school social workers and youth ministers. In a short time they can get several things done:

● Establish a directory with names and telephone numbers of school, clergy and resource personnel.

● Exchange calendars of school and church activities for teenagers.

● Discuss the kind of information appropriate to be shared between church and school staff.

● Agree on guidelines for confidentiality when a student comes to a counselor or youth minister with a problem.

● Develop a face-to-face familiarity with other youth workers. These relationships lay the groundwork for future consultation to help particular students or families. This opportunity is particularly valuable for school and church personnel new to the community.

In one community, such an exchange of information helped when it came time, some weeks later, to deal with Heather.

Clearly, something strange had happened to Heather between seventh and eighth grades. Torn jeans, the same dirty black denim jacket every day, heavy metal jewelry, and unkempt hair were a noticeable change from her appearance in seventh grade. Profanity and two smoking infractions brought her to the attention of the assistant principal and then the counselor.

Because the counselor had developed a working relationship with the youth minister at Heather's church, the two shared observations and insights. Heather had also been showing rebellion at church. Though her parents drove her each week to youth meetings, she often disappeared with a friend to the nearby bowling alley until the 9 p.m. pickup time. When she did attend meetings, she was alternately sullen and argumentative. The youth minister also remembered how deeply embarrassed Heather was when, during an overnight church lock-in, her parents arrived to check on her at 10:30 p.m.

The youth minister had discussed Heather's erratic attendance and behavior with her parents, but without apparent effect. Both were active in church affairs—her mother was congregation president—and the youth minister didn't want to push too hard. But with the additional information from the school (and with the parents' knowledge that he was communicating with the school), the youth minister began regular counseling sessions with Heather's parents. Some sessions included Heather.

Gradually, reluctantly, the parents began to ease their restrictive and protective parenting practices. And gradually Heather began to exhibit more acceptable dress and behavior. Though Heather's participation in the youth group was never enthusiastic, it became more regular and less argumentative and sullen.

Share expertise. Churches and schools can also cooperate by sharing expertise. Some youth ministers with particular skills in sports or drama, for example, volunteer to share those skills with schools that can't afford to hire enough coaches or drama teachers. While these youth workers avoid specifically religious activities in schools, they consider their work there a ministry as they support young people, get to know them and get them to feel comfortable being around a minister.

Similarly, educators can offer valuable resources for church programming. For example, teachers and counselors can be valuable leaders for workshops, meetings and retreats. They can share their expertise in a particular field, and they can share their insights about adolescence based on their training and their daily contact with hundreds of teenagers. Some may even be willing to help with special projects. For example, a wood shop teacher could be a valuable resource when preparing a youth group for a summer workcamp to build or refurbish homes for the poor.

Visit one another's events. Some church youth workers frequently visit after-school sports practice, athletic contests, evening plays and musical productions, and school award ceremonies (with the permission and blessing of school personnel when appropriate). These ministers know

"I didn't expect to see you here tonight,
Mrs. Rodriguez . . ."

how important it is for teenagers to know that their youth worker genuinely cares about them and is interested in all areas of their lives—not just what they do on Wednesday and Sunday.

Teenagers are equally delighted to see a school person at the church carnival, variety show or youth choir concert. "How come you're here?" was Andy's excited question to his school counselor (not a member of that church) at intermission of the church youth musical. When the counselor replied, "To see you," Andy was incredulous. He walked away radiating delight. The counselor later heard from Andy's parents what a tremendous lift it had been to Andy's spirits that the counselor cared that much about him.

Parents Can Make It Happen

It's easy for school teachers and administrators and for church pastors and youth workers to get so wrapped up in their own work that they forget about (or are annoyed with) the schedules of other institutions interested in teenagers. Parents who want to keep communication open between church and school should take the initiative in seeing that it happens.

Parents who hold membership and influence in both the church and school can serve both institutions by keeping them aware of each other and helping them work, day to day, as partners—not competitors for teenagers' time, attention and loyalty.

If church and school aren't communicating as much as you wish, say so. Volunteer to help pass information between them. Seek counseling and conferences with the professionals in each setting when questions or difficulties arise. Encourage people in each institution to talk with one another. The communication will benefit your children.

The church and the public school are best described as complementary institutions. Public schools can do many valuable things that are beyond the church's scope and resources. Churches can applaud and support these efforts.

The complementary relationship works the other way too. Because of the important church-state separation in American life, churches can do many things that schools can't and shouldn't do. Churches can work in areas of character development and spiritual identity that most schools are reluctant to touch. Yet schools can receive and appreciate the benefits of that development when they deal with enthusiastic and positive students who are secure in their identity and hold values that affirm the good in life.

CHAPTER 12

Educating Your Royal Child

Suppose you were given one of the children of the British royal family to care for during the growing-up years. And suppose you were expected to return this child to the palace at, say, age 20. You'd probably feel privileged to be chosen for the task. You'd take it on quite solemnly, and the prospect of the child's eventual return to the palace would introduce a note of sadness into some of your reflective moments.

How would raising a royal child affect your goals? What parenting guidelines might you construct for yourself? What would you provide? What would you permit? What would you encourage? What would you discourage? More to the point: What would you expect at school? What would you hope for in the child's education?

And what if your teenager is that royal child?

In the Christian view, nothing we have is entirely and finally ours. Our lives are given to us as gifts from God. Our talents, history, heritage and circumstances are also gifts.

So are our children. In the ultimate sense, they belong neither to us nor to themselves, but to God. To be sure, if we are biological parents, we were involved in the miracle of their creation. But—no matter how they came to us— they are not ultimately ours. They are God's.

Therefore, the young people in our houses—the ones we feed peanut butter sandwiches to, tell our spouse stories

about, give lectures to, hug, laugh at and discipline—are
members of God's royal family. As Peter said in his letter to
the Christians in Asia Minor: "But you are a chosen people,
a royal priesthood, a holy nation, a people belonging to
God, that you may declare the praises of him who called
you out of darkness into his wonderful light" (1 Peter 2:9).

We strongly suspect that thinking of your child as
royalty would shift the focus from grades and competition
in school to other emphases. Royal children don't have to
prove that they're smarter than other students or that they
can beat others in athletics or music. Royalty don't need to
pin success or failure on the symbolic grade. Their education is more likely to be guided by the end results, not by
whether they arrive ahead of the pack at each milestone
along the way.

When you understand your teenager's royal identity as
a child of the King, it changes the way you think. Getting
your teenager to raise the grade in civics from a D to a C
next term may still be a goal. But it will have less importance than, say, evidence of a sense of responsibility or a
tendency to look after those who are younger, weaker or
less able.

A desire for improved grades doesn't go away when
you think of your child as royalty, but it's joined by a
crowd of other hopes and goals—some of them more
valuable than high grades. What's more, in most of these
hopes you are not only a teacher but a co-learner with
your teenager.

What do children of royalty need to know and learn as
they grow up? And, if indeed your teenager is part of the
King's family, how do some of the following goals for
royalty influence what you hope your child will learn as he
or she grows up? ("The Other Report Card" in the Appen-
dix is a practical activity you can use with your teenager to
explore these goals.)

A Sense of Royal Identity

Children of royalty need, above all else, a sense of their royal identity. You'd want your child to know that royalty is dedicated to the unique purposes of being a major symbol of national identity. You'd help the child find his or her own expression of that purpose. But no one would question that there is such a purpose.

One of the most essential things you can do for your teenager is to foster the sense of self-esteem that comes from knowing what it means to be a child of God. Of all other aspects of your teenager's education, that goal is most basic. Teenagers' spiritual identity is the spring from which everything else—values, motivations, behavior—arises.

You don't have to use a hammer to pound it in, nor use a lot of words. All of us find out who we are by the way people speak to us and what they expect of us—by who *they* think we are.

Reflect on that. By our tone of voice and words, every time we speak, we shape a teenager's identity in tiny increments. "Child of God, it's study time." "Child of God, you'll want to remember your math book today." You don't have to *say* that, but *think* it now and then.

Further, your child needs a sense of purpose in life. Psychologists and educators are currently debating whether the major influence in life is a sense of self-esteem (which is what most people think) or whether it is, instead, a sense of purpose. Perhaps one leads to the other. Teenagers who are fully convinced of their child-of-Godness will search out their own expression of their life's purpose. But they won't doubt that there is a purpose.

 ## *A* Sense of Respect

The royal student would be taught to respect everyone. Members of the royal family must be able to talk with people who have no particular social status as well as

*those of considerable wealth and position. You'd encour-
age the child to meet and grow fond of many different
kinds of people. Surely any evidence in a royal child of
putting down or discounting anyone would be dealt with
sternly. Putdowns almost always rise from a lack of secure
identity. Being who they are, royalty don't need to elevate
themselves by devaluing others.*

A step in the direction of helping teenagers develop
respect for everyone is to see that they become acquainted
with a wide variety of people—young and old, poor and
not-so-poor, people who are quick of mind, people who
think slowly.

But acquaintance is not enough; the aim is higher.
Being a child of God confers the belief that the smelly boy
whose locker is next to your teenager's is just as dear and
valuable to God as your teenager is.

You foster or retard that belief in your teenager day in
and day out by the way you talk about your friends and
your teenager's friends. Ask yourself if your own actions
and words convey respect of others:

● Whom do you seek out at the church social hour?
Mainly those with "position"? Or some of the less
splendidly dressed people? Or those who are strangers?

● Do you show respect in dealing with your teenager
by giving him or her the right of privacy?

● Are you able to avoid the superior-subordinate
posture in making requests and inquiries of your teenager?

 ## *A* Sense of the Difference Between the Fake and the Real

*A royal child needs to learn to separate the fake from
the real. Perhaps we should call it "acquiring good taste."
Certainly a prince or princess should be well-acquainted
with the arts, knowing how to distinguish excellence in
each of them. The child's education should also foster an
ability to distinguish the fake from the real in relationships. A royal person must be able to distinguish*

manipulative attention from real friendship.

Learning to separate the fake from the real—in art, manufactured products and people—is important for your teenager too. This educational goal is a good thing to keep in mind when your teenager chooses school electives. One characteristic of a good general education is that it gives learners some standards for appreciation in fields where they probably will never become expert.

Such an education encourages familiarity with illustrations of excellence. Dorothy remembers with amazement and gratitude the teacher who played recordings of grand opera and Debussy's "Afternoon of a Faun" for a handful of Depression-era ninth-graders, helping them identify instruments and follow musical themes. Those ninth-graders from northern Minnesota grew up to be farmers, ore boat workers, teachers, garage mechanics, homemakers but, as far as we know, no musicians. Yet they all have, safely stored in their memories, the sound of that opening flute solo of "Faun."

Even though the teenager may never become a confirmed concert-goer, haunter of art galleries or an avid reader, illustrations of excellence furnish the mind with sounds and images that influence subsequent seeing, hearing and thinking. They stock the mind with references that enable us to make better sense of what people say, ask, propose or show. As a result we can build richer connections with other people and with life's expectations.

Separating the fake from the real in friendship is also important. Genuine friendships don't exploit, but are trustworthy. Your own royal child needs to discover—sometimes through painful experience—what characteristics distinguish fake friendships from real.

The media would have us believe that we can trust particular products to make us attractive and influential. But that kind of attractiveness and influence is mostly illusion. Keep an eye out for signs that your teenager has stopped believing those fairy-tale promises. And celebrate when you see that your teenager has begun to learn some of the gracious humility that shows itself in expressed appreciation and consideration of others' interests. These are the traits of genuine friendships.

🍎 *A* Sense of Responsibility

Another part of royal training leads toward a sense of responsibility for others. A royal child must learn to recognize other people's rights to speak the truth, and to hear that truth even when the message is unpleasant. Sometimes royalty must recognize that people for whom they are responsible aren't receiving proper attention. They need to hear the uncomfortable word that some people are in need, and then take steps to correct the problem.

For too long we have lived in a culture where "me first" has been not only lived, but promoted by the media and advertisers as desirable: "Take care of yourself!" "You deserve it!" "You're #1!"

But there's another, more important dimension of life that's based on self-forgetfulness—not self-consciousness. A good education will accustom your child to observing what others need, and doing what he or she can to help.

This perspective is often learned by observation too. Your own availability for volunteer work from time to time, says it. Your own capacity to see what needs to be done in a situation, and then doing it, also teaches. And your teenager learns to contribute to a group's welfare when home chores are considered the joint responsibility of everyone who lives there.

🍎 *A* Strong Desire for Justice

A future monarch needs to learn how to set in motion forces to work toward justice, no matter how unpopular that decision might be. It would be important for such a child to "hunger and thirst for righteousness"—to have a desire for justice that can survive the disapproval of others.

Illustration of justice begins at home. You teach justice when you listen respectfully to your teenager's objection to something you've asked for. Regardless of the discussion's final outcome, careful listening is justice illustrated.

Lack of justice plagues our world, and the pity is that we become so used to it that we think injustice is normal. Teenagers with a strong sense of justice nearly always come from homes where parents themselves are caught up in talk and action that serve justice. These parents may be involved in, for example, fighting discrimination, championing preservation of the Earth's resources, or defending the rights of children or the elderly who can't speak for themselves. Whatever the specific issue, families teach the attitude of concern for justice in the world.

A Sense of Stewardship

A royal child should be able to distinguish the significant from the insignificant and set sensible priorities. Even royal status gives no more than 24 hours per day, and invariably there are more demands for the royal family's time than there are hours available. However many hordes of advisers there may be, only the monarch can make the final judgments.

It's important for our own children of God to be able to set their own priorities (within reasonable limits) in use of time, in attention, in spending money. Although we can't assume our children's interests will always coincide with our own, it's sometimes all right to ask, "Is this really as important as you're making it seem?" If an activity helps your teenager distinguish the important from the unimportant, it serves a useful educational purpose.

Like many other values, stewardship is also taught by example. Do you allow hours of television to gobble up time you had fully intended to spend on something more lasting? Does your giving to church and charitable causes come off the top of your resources, or must it compete with everything else in the budget? Although you may never specifically discuss those topics, your teenagers are learning from what you do, nevertheless.

🍎 Respect and Desire for Knowledge

Respect and desire for knowledge would also be an essential component of a royal child's education. A broad knowledge of the world is an important part of education—as is a willingness and desire to seek information when it isn't immediately available.

Up through high school, formal education should embrace as wide a spectrum of learning as possible. There's time enough later for specialized learning. Our teenagers should understand why all schools require a broad range of courses. "Because the state Department of Education says so," is too shallow an answer, even though true.

To understand their place in the known world, our royal children need at least a foundational knowledge of that world. Everyone should understand how history, geography, music, science, language, math and all the rest help us move about more knowledgeably and make better decisions. Besides, understanding the purpose of knowledge is an important factor in motivation.

As parents, we sometimes naturally assume our children will take on our own enthusiasms and interests. Sometimes they do, but not all children of avid gardeners turn out to be avid gardeners. If your children have interests in areas of knowledge different from your own, encourage and support them. It isn't necessarily a waste of time for your teenager to pore for hours over baseball trading cards. He or she is exploring an area of knowledge outside yours. Why not learn from him or her?

If you talk with parents of adult children about their children's interests, you'll discover how the parents' worlds have expanded because of what their children enjoy. We know a psychologist whose son competes in body-building, as well as a family of gymnasts whose daughter is deeply involved in community theater.

We've enjoyed our own introduction to the world of international barbershop competition through our son who conducts a barbershop chorus. And we've become acquainted with formula-car racing because our daughter is a trained race track corner worker (a volunteer function that increases the drivers' safety). We often find ourselves able to converse easily with people we've newly met because we know a little about whole areas of endeavor that we once scarcely knew existed until a child introduced them to us.

🍎 Self-Discipline

A royal child's complaints about a particular school, course or assignment would be sympathetically heard and appropriately examined. But it's unlikely that such complaints would, by themselves, serve as grounds for switching schools, changing courses or negotiating out of assignments.

Gordonstoun is a boys school in Scotland specializing—so news stories report—in early morning runs and cold showers before breakfast. Both Prince Charles and Prince Andrew attended the boarding school beginning at age 13. While Prince Andrew enjoyed Gordonstoun, chroniclers of British royalty agree that "Prince Charles was unhappy at school, being neither an outstanding scholar nor . . . a natural leader."[1] We aren't told whether Charles ever asked to be transferred out of the school, but we do know he remained there until graduation. A certain amount of self-discipline is expected of a future king.

The range of normal teenage behavior is from squirrely to serene, from monstrous to meditative. Parents must understand and accept that. But we also need to help our children develop a sense of what's appropriate in different situations. Self-discipline controls behavior—not so that it's always "adult behavior," but so that it's appropriate.

The combination of sense of appropriateness and self-discipline is what gets home chores done, whether the teenager or adult is doing them. It also gets homework done, whether it's school-related homework or the stuff a parent carried home in a briefcase. It governs punctuality, healthy sleeping patterns and junk-food consumption. It never stops being essential, even for adults. Your teenager needs to know that.

*A*bility to Know When Enough Work Is Enough

Royalty must be educated to take people and issues seriously and attend to them carefully. But royalty must also be able to let go of the burdens of monarchy and go horseback riding, play games, laugh with friends or curl up in a corner to read.

Mental health experts say we must develop the right balance of "mindwork" and "mindrest." No matter our age, we need to find and to live that balance.

When a teenager sees hard-working parents schedule regular time for tennis or digging in the garden, an example of balance between work and play registers. The point is further clarified when a parent refuses to allow work to intrude on family traditions such as church attendance, family birthday celebrations and holiday gatherings.

Television and reading are both (when carefully monitored) perfectly acceptable ways to "smell the flowers." But there's a considerable difference between a planned and purposeful use of television, and letting the television seduce you into several hours of glassy-eyed staring during time you had intended to use on projects of more lasting value.

*O*ther Goals, Other Yardsticks

These long-term goals and values aren't how many parents think of education. But thinking of the kinds of "grades" that are important for a royal child can do several things. First, it tells your teenager that you no longer pin all your hopes on the academic, sports or arts performance that constitute the usual "field of play." It gives greater weight to the quality of the person rather than to the prizes won or the visible results produced. And it might also bring you and your teenager closer together than ever before.

There is one other matter too. If you were educating royalty, you'd want to be in touch with the palace to report on how things are going, talk about what troubles or puzzles you, and ask for guidance.

Even so. Prayer.

Prayer need not always be a specific petition, though it often is. One form of intercessory prayer is to enter God's presence, mentally standing with your hand on your teenager's shoulder and waiting. Perhaps you review before God your recent history with your child. Or perhaps you say, "I would like to know how best to help my teenager grow within your will."

And then you wait.

Perhaps you receive a message. Perhaps you only enter the Presence and wait. It's our experience that whether you receive an identifiable message or simply wait, that kind of prayer changes your perspective on your teenager.

And it changes you as well.

 AFTERWORD

Our Education as Parents

If you keep your eyes and ears open, life provides non-stop education. It doesn't cease when your fingers close around your final diploma. It goes on throughout life. Parenthood is one of the most thorough and exacting of educations, brimful of discoveries and chastening evidence that one needs to learn still more. Thus it's a spur to humility.

Being a good parent is more difficult than most parents anticipate. It's more rewarding too, of course, but it's more difficult.

Images of Parenthood

If our experience is typical, young people think in two separate age categories when they anticipate having children: first, the sweet, tender look and touch of babyhood up to about age 4 or 5. Second, the healthy, lively age of late high school and beyond—from about 17 to 22. They think about happy baby sounds, curly heads, tiny arms hugging trustfully, the endearing ineptitudes of toddlerhood, the warmth of a small, weary head cuddled on your shoulder. Then their minds jump immediately to see clear-eyed, principled, promising competence in a charming and appreciative young adult. What they don't think about is what comes between. That's where a great deal of the difficulty—and hence the learning—lies.

Not all the learning takes place in between, of course. It starts earlier. During the first month or so of a baby's existence, parents discover that life has irrevocably changed. Demands now present themselves regularly, without regard for your own convenience or comfort. The inescapability of the 2 a.m. feeding, followed by on-call duty at any time of day or night, becomes an accepted part of the routine. Your child's needs are one of the fixed points around which you arrange the rest of life.

In healthy marriages, these experiences leave their positive mark. A new kind of patience and an increased capacity for responsibility show themselves. Often the changes aren't visible to you until someone else points them out. And then you smile in recognition.

Other learning follows. More and more often you discover that your child uses a tone of voice, repeats an expression, or makes a gesture that's uncannily like you. You're startled by how powerfully your unexamined doings and sayings have become instruments of instruction. You're teaching all the time—even when you're not thinking about it. Thoughtful parents often make the logical leap and assume, quite correctly, that they're also teaching things that haven't yet appeared in imitated form, but that are being learned nevertheless.

After you recover from the startling discovery of seeing yourself mirrored in your child, you sometimes make changes—changes in intention, changes in habits. And if the changes are real, those changes—like those before them—constitute another step in maturity.

Learning Through Adolescence

In about seventh or eighth grade, hints of what your child has learned over the past 13 or 14 years begin to become evident. In some cases, pleasantly evident. In others, troublingly so.

Some years ago, both of us taught Parent Effectiveness Training courses. The course is designed for parents of children of any age, so all our classes included variety—a sprinkling of brand-new parents, some with children in grade school, some in high school and, more often than you might think, people with adult children. We discovered that parents of junior and senior highers were the ones who came with the most urgent, real questions and the greatest eagerness to learn new skills.

It's easy to see why.

At the secondary school age it becomes obvious to both the teenager and the parent that the child is no longer a child. In effect, the style of thinking, the physical power and the amount of freedom the young person has are altering the relationship between parent and child.

In families where parents used power and authority to shape their children's learning habits, some new ways of relating, some new persuasional skills and some new understandings of the parent-child relationship must be absorbed and practiced.

It's difficult. But difficulty, when worked through, is often redemptive. Just as the 2 a.m. feedings and the late-night calls for medical advice made you a different person, so also can you grow by developing the new skills you need in order to continue to be a successful parent to your growing teenager.

This stage of growth will continue to change your ways of relating not only to your teenager but to everyone, as well as your ways of thinking about yourself. However, as Jesus implied, the best changes in you occur when you're not thinking about yourself, but about somebody else.

There are four things parents of teenagers discover about their role in their teenager's life, beginning about the time their teenager enters secondary school:

1. The first learning occurs when you catch sight—as a feeling in your bones, not an intellectual concept—of the fact that this child is actually going to be an adult one day. You've known it all along, of course. But one day it becomes real, and that shifts your focus a little.

2. A second thing happens as your teenager becomes

increasingly able to seek information, make friends and acquire money on his or her own: You have less and less direct power. At one time, this child was entirely dependent on you for everything—food, clothing, direction, advice, approval, companionship. But those days are gone. Alert to that shift, you find that you express more of your wishes as requests rather than demands. You recognize your teenager's ability to take or leave your advice, so you give fewer orders and make more suggestions. You begin to guide, not direct.

3. A third thing that happens is that you become more aware of your teenager's spiritual identity. Many denominations devote the early teenage years to studying the family's religious tradition and making decisions for or against accepting that faith as one's own. The learning your teenager has absorbed, largely from you, about his or her spiritual identity is crucial to the decision—and to the subsequent life-view that teenager takes as an adult.

This is a trying time. Teenagers ask new questions that we don't have instant answers for—and they insist on answers. We don't need to know everything. Our challenge is to acknowledge the difficulty of the questions and offer any partial and provisional answers we may have.

British theologian Leslie Weatherhead suggests a helpful concept.[1] He says there are certain difficult questions he turns over in his mind, examines carefully, then places in a mental drawer labeled "awaiting further light."

The Christian faith has much mystery in it. Some of the questions your teenager asks are questions Christian thinkers have puzzled over for ages. You needn't come up with a definitive response between 4:00 and 4:05 p.m. on any given afternoon. We're all "awaiting further light." In the meantime, we rely on our trust in the God who has carried us safe thus far, and has so often demonstrated his love.

4. There is yet a fourth learning that occurred for us somewhat later than our children's high school years. It also has been a valuable part of our learning. Once you have a child, the welfare of that child—no matter his or her age—never ceases to be of great importance to you. And you'll never cease to be vulnerable to the doings, struggles, anxieties, mistakes and troubles your child encounters. They will always have the capacity to hurt you. Sometimes to delight you, of course. But also to hurt you. And you have no defense against it.

What have we learned from that insight? It has given us an inkling of the greatness of the gift God gave us when he conferred free will. For we understand now that we can never say to God, like rebellious teenagers, "It's none of your business what I do." That's one freedom not included in the package. Our children can never move far enough away from us that we're no longer vulnerable to their pain. Similarly, we can never escape God's sight and care and love, nor the knowledge that we can and do cause God pain. There's something life-altering about that discovery.

 ## The Most Valuable Education

Are these discoveries worth what it costs every parent to make them? "Worth" (as for something bought or sold) loses its meaning in this context. We don't know how to answer the question. Nobody would ask for the kind of trouble having children brings unless it brought with it something else of value.

Being parents is one of the greatest educations we've ever had. It's been rewarding. It's been difficult. And we sometimes think that our learnings when our children were teenagers gave us the best education of all. We sincerely hope the same for you. And we hope your teenagers succeed in living a life in which their education never really stops, their understanding of you grows, and your love for each other is rewarding beyond all you have ever hoped.

 APPENDIX

The Other Report Card

The form on page 184 (Diagram 5, "The Other Report Card") is intended for you and your teenager to use together to think about the nine goals listed in Chapter 12. (For example, questions 1 through 4 refer to "A Sense of Royal Identity.")

Before using "The Other Report Card," discuss the qualities in the chapter together, and talk about whether your teenager would like to use the form with you. Make it clear that you intend your teenager to rate you, just as you will rate your teenager.

If your teenager agrees, decide on a time period during which you'll observe each other, starting now. Before you start, decide which characteristics you'll watch for. You may leave the form as it is; you may add some character-istics in the blank spaces at the bottom; or you may decide to rate only three or four of the qualities mentioned.

Use the form each time school grades are issued, every six months or once a year on the teenager's birthday—whichever you choose. Make two copies of the form. Each of you will assign ratings for the other on one copy. When the observation period has ended, do your rating separately. Then talk about the "grades." If you can, give examples you've seen to support your ratings. Talk about what you believe affects the person's behavior in the area—and anything else you wish. Be sure you use the questions at the end of the form to talk about how you felt about the discussion before you close your conversation.

Though the discussion of the form may seem unusually heavy, it will help you talk about values and spiritual identity—those levels of reality that teenagers and their parents so seldom discuss. It will also reinforce for both of you the reality that grades are not the only goal in life worth pursuing, nor the only standard for success.

Diagram 5
The Other Report Card

This report card is about_____

as observed by_____

during the (past term, past month, past six months, past year).

Date of rating: _____

Directions: For each of the personal qualities listed below, circle the number that best describes what you have observed about this person during the period indicated.

	Low evidence			High evidence
1. Feeling good about yourself.	1	2	3	4	5
2. Recognizing and using the talents God has given you.	1	2	3	4	5
3. Feeling a sense of purpose in life.	1	2	3	4	5
4. Praying for help in making decisions.	1	2	3	4	5
5. Complimenting or encouraging others.	1	2	3	4	5
6. Respecting others' rights.	1	2	3	4	5
7. Paying attention to people others ignore.	1	2	3	4	5
8. Making thoughtful choices; choosing things of real value.	1	2	3	4	5
9. Showing friendship in creative ways.	1	2	3	4	5
10. Doing things for others without being asked.	1	2	3	4	5
11. Taking leadership when it's appropriate.	1	2	3	4	5

	Low evidence			High evidence	
12. Praying for others.	1	2	3	4	5
13. Telling the truth.	1	2	3	4	5
14. Respecting rules and laws.	1	2	3	4	5
15. Standing up for an unpopular person or idea.	1	2	3	4	5
16. Using time wisely.	1	2	3	4	5
17. Using money wisely.	1	2	3	4	5
18. Paying attention to important things; not fussing over unimportant things.	1	2	3	4	5
19. Being curious about a lot of different things.	1	2	3	4	5
20. Showing interest in others' activities and accomplishments.	1	2	3	4	5
21. Following through with what you start.	1	2	3	4	5
22. Doing things that need to be done but that you don't like to do.	1	2	3	4	5
23. Doing what you say you'll do for others.	1	2	3	4	5
24. Taking responsibility for your own work, messes and mistakes.	1	2	3	4	5
25. Being able to laugh at your own goofs.	1	2	3	4	5
26. Taking time to relax and enjoy yourself.	1	2	3	4	5
27. Taking regular time for meditation, reading and prayer.	1	2	3	4	5
28. _____	1	2	3	4	5
29. _____	1	2	3	4	5
30. _____	1	2	3	4	5

Continued

Talk together about your markings:

1. Does the person being rated think the ratings are fair?

2. Which ratings does this person think should be changed?

3. What evidence of the characteristic has the rater seen?

4. Record any specific changes the person being rated wants to

make: _____

_____

About your discussion:

1. Did either of you get angry?

2. Who did most of the talking?

3. Was either of you resentful of the activity or the time it took?

4. How does each of you feel about the conversation?

5. Decide whether you want to have another rating time, and when. Write it on your family calendar.

ENDNOTES

Chapter 1

[1]Peter Benson, Dorothy Williams and Arthur Johnson, *The Quicksilver Years: The Hopes and Fears of Early Adolescence* (San Francisco, CA: Harper & Row, 1987), p. 64.

[2]Group Publishing survey of 520 parents of teenagers, reported in Eugene C. Roehlkepartain (editor), *The Youth Ministry Resource Book* (Loveland, CO: Group Books, 1988), p. 164.

[3]*What Works: Research About Teaching and Learning* (Washington, DC: U.S. Department of Education, 1986), p. 7.

[4]Bruno Bettelheim, *A Good Enough Parent: A Book on Child Rearing* (New York, NY: Knopf, 1987), p. 55.

[5]National Commission on Excellence in Education. *A Nation at Risk: The Imperative for Educational Reform* (Washington, DC: U.S. Department of Education, 1983), p. 35.

[6]Benson et al., p. 93.

[7]C.S. Lewis, *Mere Christianity* (New York, NY: Macmillan, 1978), p. 99.

Chapter 2

[1]National Commission on Excellence in Education, p. 27.

[2]Richard J. Stiggins, "Revitalizing Classroom Assessment: The Highest Instructional Priority," Phi Delta Kappa (January 1988), p. 365.

[3]Robert McAfee Brown, "Speaking About Israel: Some Ground Rules," The Christian Century (April 6, 1988), p. 339.

[4]Eric Hoffer, *The Ordeal of Change* (New York, NY: Harper & Row, 1952), p. 5.

Chapter 3

[1]Benson et al., p. 64.

[2]John M. Goldenring and Ronald Doctor, "California Adolescents' Concerns About the Threat of Nuclear War" (unpublished paper presented to the Third International Symposium of the International Physicians for the Prevention of Nuclear War, Helsinki, Finland, June 1984).

[3]Benson et al., p. 93.

[4]Benson et al., p. 173.

Chapter 6

[1]Benson et al., p. 189.

[2]Benson et al., p. 190.

[3]Bettelheim, p. 62.

[4]Bettelheim, p. 56.

Chapter 7

[1]Benson et al., p. 15.

[2]James S. Coleman, Thomas Hoffer and Sally Kilgore, *High School Achievement: Public, Catholic and Private Schools Compared* (New York, NY: Basic Books, 1982), p. 104.

[3]Tony Buzan, *Use Both Sides of Your Brain* (New York, NY: E.P. Dutton, 1976), p. 55.

[4]Ibid.

Chapter 8

[1]"The Gallup Poll of Teachers' Attitudes Toward the Public Schools," Phi Delta Kappan (October 1984), p. 104.

Chapter 10

[1]Ellen Greenberger and Laurence Steinberg, *When Teenagers Work: The Psychological and Social Costs of Adolescent Employment* (New York, NY: Basic Books, 1986), p. 15-16.

[2]David L. Clark, "High School Seniors React to Their Teachers and Their Schools," Phi Delta Kappan (March 1987), p. 508.

[3]Greenberger and Steinberg, p. 248.

[4]Jerald D. Bachman, Lloyd D. Johnston and Patrick M. O'Malley, *Monitoring the Future 1986* (Ann Arbor, MI: Institute for Social Research, University of Michigan, 1987), p. 195-196.

[5]Greenberger and Steinberg, p. 141.

[6]Bachman et al., p. 196.

Chapter 11

[1]U.S. Supreme Court decision in *Abington School District v. Schempp,* quoted in *Religion in the Public School Classroom* (Washington, DC: Baptist Joint Committee on Public Affairs, n.d.).

[2]Ibid.

[3]Peter L. Benson, Phillip K. Wood, Arthur L. Johnson, Carolyn H. Eklin and Janice E. Mills, *Report on 1983 Minnesota Survey on Drug Use and Drug-Related Attitudes* (Minneapolis, MN: Search Institute, 1983), p. 100.

Chapter 12

[1]Donald Edgar, *Britain's Royal Family in the Twentieth Century* (New York, NY: Crown Publishers in the U.S.A., 1979), p. 162.

Afterword

[1]Leslie Weatherhead, *The Christian Agnostic* (Nashville, TN: Abingdon Press, 1979), p. 21.

Practical help for parents of teenagers from

Group®

What Makes Your Teenager Tick
Dr. G. Keith Olson

Here's practical Christian help for every parent who has ever been baffled by their teenager's behavior.

With this easy-to-read guide you'll explore the personality of your teenager, plus how to react . . . how to discipline . . . and how to nurture.

Bring out the best in your kid. This complete resource will teach you how to:

- Turn your teenager's weaknesses into strengths
- Help your adolescent get along better with others
- Support your teenager in positive, creative ways
- Help your teenager grow into a mature, Christian adult

You will find *What Makes Your Teenager Tick* perfect for better understanding your adolescent's personality. And through understanding, you'll build a strong, positive relationship with your teenager—to last a lifetime.

Adapted from the best-selling book Why Teenagers Act the Way They Do.
Family Tree™
ISBN 0-931529-75-1, $8.95

Parenting Teenagers
Video kit

Parents will find needed support for coping with their teenagers—through practical video training.

Get the insights and encouragement you need from *Parenting Teenagers*. You'll discover practical communication tips, the whys of rebellion, insights on mood swings, ideas for handling peer pressure . . . plus parenting styles, kids' friends and more.

Watch *Parenting Teenagers* at home, or use for years to come in parents meetings, retreats or Sunday school.

Your complete kit includes four 30-minute VHS videos and 144-page information-packed leaders guide full of helpful, ready-to-copy worksheets. Discover . . .

Video 1: What Makes Your Teenager Tick?
Video 2: Parenting: How Do You Rate?
Video 3: Communicating With Your Teenager
Video 4: Your Teenager's Friends and Peer Pressure

Get the support you need to survive the tough teenage years.

Group Books
ISBN 0-931529-60-3, $98

Student Plan-It Calendar
Daily Organizer

Help your teenagers stay focused on Christ—and manage their busy schedules. Students will love this week-at-a-glance devotional calendar. It's appealing and fun to use—a great date-keeper! Students will use it to keep track of . . .

- Class and work schedules
- Addresses and phone numbers
- After-school activities
- Special dates
- Assignments
- Reminders

The *Student Plan-It Calendar* is all busy teenagers need to organize their time. This nifty organizer puts kids in charge of their busy schedules. Plus, scripture verses and weekly devotions encourage positive, Christian attitudes in students.

Encourage faith and self-discipline when you give your student this colorful, easy-to-tote devotional for graduation or as a back-to-school gift.

Teenage Books™
$6.95

PARENTS & TEENAGERS
Newsletter

Discover easy-to-use ideas and support—to make parenting teenagers less stressful. Easier. And fun!

In each issue of *PARENTS & TEENAGERS*, you'll get . . .

- Tips on how to improve communication with your teenager
- Clues for handling crises
- Creative ways for saying "I love you"
- Helpful reviews of current movies and music
- Insights into teenage behavior
- What to do when teenagers challenge family values
- Help for coping when kids rebel, and more

Order the newsletter that's packed with encouragement and creative parenting ideas today.

2-year single subscription, $34.00
1-year single subscription (6 issues), $18.97

These and other GROUP books, videos and magazines are available at your local Christian bookstore, or order direct from the publisher: GROUP, Box 481, Loveland, CO 80539. Please add the following postage/handling fee to all direct orders: $2.50 for book orders, $4 for video orders, no postage/handling fee for magazine orders. Colorado residents add 3% sales tax.